A to Z

GTA CHEATS

12 Platforms

PC 4
    Grand Theft Auto 4
    Grand Theft Auto: London 1969 5
    Grand Theft Auto 2 7
    Grand Theft Auto 3 9
    Grand Theft Auto Vice City 11
    Grand Theft Auto SanAndreas 14
    Grand Theft Auto: THE LOST AND DAMNED 21
    Grand Theft Auto THE BALLAD OF GAY TONY 22
    Grand Theft Auto 4 24
    Grand Theft Auto Episodes From Liberty City 25
    Grand Theft Auto 5 27

PSP 32
    Grand Theft Auto: Liberty City Stories 32
    Grand Theft Auto: Vice City Stories 35
    Grand Theft Auto: Chinatown Wars 37

PSOne 38
    Grand Theft Auto 38
    Grand Theft Auto: London 1969 40
    Grand Theft Auto 2 42

PS2 44
    Grand Theft Auto 3 44
    Grand Theft Auto Vice City 46
    Grand Theft Auto SanAndreas 49
    Grand Theft Auto: Liberty City Stories 55
    Grand Theft Auto: Vice City Stories 57

PS3 59
    Grand Theft Auto SanAndreas 59
    Grand Theft Auto: THE LOST AND DAMNED 64
    Grand Theft Auto THE BALLAD OF GAY TONY 65

Grand Theft Auto 4	67
Grand Theft Auto Episodes From Liberty City	69
Grand Theft Auto 5	72
PS4	**74**
Grand Theft Auto 5	74
Xbox	**78**
Grand Theft Auto 3	78
Grand Theft Auto Vice City	81
Grand Theft Auto SanAndreas	86
Xbox One	**92**
Grand Theft Auto 5	92
Xbox 360	**94**
Grand Theft Auto SanAndreas	94
Grand Theft Auto: THE LOST AND DAMNED	99
Grand Theft Auto THE BALLAD OF GAY TONY	101
Grand Theft Auto 4	103
Grand Theft Auto Episodes From Liberty City	105
Grand Theft Auto 5	108
Nintendo DS	**110**
Grand Theft Auto: Chinatown Wars	110
GameBoy Advance	**112**
Grand Theft Auto ADVANCE	112
Mobile	**113**
Grand Theft Auto 3	113
Grand Theft Auto Vice City	113
Grand Theft Auto SanAndreas	113

PC

Grand Theft Auto

Enter these as your character's name to enable the cheat:

Code	Effect
heart of gold	10x Point Multiplier
hate machine	10x Point Multiplier
itcouldbeyou	9,999,999 points
satanlives	99 lives
nineinarow	All Levels
super well	All levels and Cities
itsgallus	All stages
iamnotgarypenn	Disable Massive Cursing
iamgarypenn	Enable Massive Cursing
buckfast, then press *	Get 99 ammo for all guns
iamthelaw	No police
stevesmates	No Police presence
porkcharsui	Once pressing c in game, you can see damage, speed etc of your current car in the game
suckmyrocket	Start with all weapons and power-ups
itstantrum	Unlimited Lives
6031769	Unlimited Lives

Grand Theft Auto: London 1969

Codes

Enter these as your character's name to enable the cheat:

Code	Effect
heart of gold	10x Point Multiplier
hate machine	10x Point Multiplier
itcouldbeyou	9,999,999 points
satanlives	99 lives
nineinarow	All Levels
super well	All levels and Cities
itsgallus	All stages
iamnotgarypenn	Disable Massive Cursing
iamgarypenn	Enable Massive Cursing
buckfast, then press *	Get 99 ammo for all guns
iamthelaw	No police
stevesmates	No Police presence
porkcharsui	Once pressing c in game, you can see damage, speed etc of your current car in the game
suckmyrocket	Start with all weapons and power-ups
itstantrum	Unlimited Lives
6031769	Unlimited Lives

Password Cheats

Rename your character to these passwords

Password	Effect
iamgod	10x Multiplier and All Weapons (Press *)
flashmotor	All levels unlocked
travelcard	All levels unlocked
super well	All levels unlocked
rommel	Debug mode
6661970	Infinitive lives
pieandmash	Infinitive Lives (Press * for all weapons)
driveby	Lets you fire your gun out of the window of your car
psychadelic	Lets you use the horn to change the color of your car
averyrichman	Maximum Points (999999999)
herc	Maximum Ponts, all weapons (Press *) All levels, Drive-by (Press Weapon when in car to fire weapon while driving)
iamfilth	No Cops
tithead	No Cops
deathtoall	Press * on the NUMPAD for all weapons
asawindow	Press * on the NUMPAD for all weapons
uaintnuffin	Some items and All weapons with infinite ammo
silence	Turn police radio off

Grand Theft Auto 2

Cheat Codes

Before you can enter any cheat codes, you'll first need to enable Cheat Mode. To do this, type gouranga in the Cheat Option. Now you should be able to enter any of the following cheat codes during gameplay.

Code	Effect
muchcash	$500,000
coolboy	$500,000
iamdavej	$9,999,999
segarulz	10x Point Multiplier
danisgod	200,000 Points
cutie1	99 Lives
gorefest	A Lot of Blood
tumyfrog	all bonus levels
tumyfrog	All Levels
ukgamer	all towns unlocked
forallgt	all waepons
godofgta	All Weapons
godofgta	all weapons+ammo
beefcake	brutality increases
SCHURULZ	Double Damage

Code	Effect
LASVEGAS	Elvis Clan
EATSOUP	Free Stuff
JAILBAIT	Get Out of Jail Free Card
livelong	godmode
rsjabber	godmode
MADEMAN	Have No Beef with Gangs
hunsrus	Invisibility
rsjabber	Invisibility
ARSESTAR	Keep Weapons after Death
nekkid	Naked People
losefeds	No Police
buckfast	Really Violent Citizens
wuggles	show coordinates
wuggles	Show Location
fishflap	Small Cars
voltfest	Unlimited Electrogun
flameon	Unlimited Flamethrower

Grand Theft Auto 3

Cheat Codes

GUNSGUNSGUNS = Weapon Cheat

IFIWEREARICHMAN = Money Cheat

GESUNDHEIT = Health Cheat

TURTOISE (or TORTOISE, in 1.1) = Armor Cheat

Weather Cheats:

SKINCANCERFORME = Nice Weather

ILiKESCOTLAND = Fog Thickness Level 1

ILOVESCOTLAND = Fog Thickness Level 2

PEASOUP = Fog Thickness Level 3

Pedestrian Cheats:

ITSALLGOINGMAAAD = Crazy Peds

NOBODYLIKESME = Peds Want To Kill You

WEAPONSFORALL = Peds Pack Heat (Carry Weapons)

CHITTYCHITTYBB = Flying Cars

Other Cheats:

MOREPOLICEPLEASE = Wanted Level Up

NOPOLICEPLEASE = Wanted Level Down

GIVEUSATANK = Spawn A Tank

ANICESETOFWHEELS = See-Thru Cars

CORNERSLIKEMAD = Better Driving Code

TIMEFLIESWHENYOU = Fast Gameplay

ILIKEDRESSINGUP = Change Character

BANGBANGBANG = Blow Up Cars Around You

Unknown Cheats:

NASTYLIMBCHEAT = Nastier Limb Removal?

MADWEATHER = Time Speeds Up?

BOOOOORING = Unknown (Time Slows Down?)

Grand Theft Auto Vice City

Codes Galore!

During Gameplay, type any of these cheats (note: codes are not case sensitive)

Code	Effect
MIAMITRAFFIC	Aggressive Drivers
THUGTOOLS	All "light weapon"
NUTTERTOOLS	All "heavy" weapons
PROFESSIONALTOOLS	All "medium" weapons
IWANTITPAINTEDBLACK	All cars are black
AHAIRDRESSERSCAR	All cars are pink
GREENLIGHT	All traffic lights are green
BIGBANG	Blow up nearby cars
IWANTBIGTITS	Candy Suxxx (Pornstar)
SEAWAYS	Cars can drive/hover over water
COMEFLYWITHME	Cars can fly
STILLLIKEDRESSINGUP	Change Skin/Clothes
ICANTTAKEITANYMORE	Commit Suicide
LEAVEMEALONE	Decrease Wanted Level
ABITDRIEG	Dense Clouds
AIRSHIP	Fast boats can fly for short periods of time
CANTSEEATHING	Foggy Weather
PRECIOUSPROTECTION	Full Armor

Code	Effect
ASPIRINE	Full Health
CHICKSWITHGUNS	Girls Carry Guns
PROGRAMMER	Gives Tommy girly arms/legs
FANNYMAGNET	Ladies Man, Women Follow You
APLEASANTDAY	Light Clouds
ONSPEED	Makes everything faster
BOOOOOORING	Makes everything slower
DEEPFRIEDMARSBARS	Makes Tommy fatter
CERTAINDEATH	Makes you smoke a cigarette
WHEELSAREALLINEED	Only the wheels of a car are visible
OURGODGIVENRIGHTTOBEARARMS	Peds Carry Guns
NOBODYLIKESME	Peds Hate You
FIGHTFIGHTFIGHT	Peds Riot
GRIPISEVERYTHING	Perfect Handling
ILOOKLIKEHILARY	Play as Hilary King
MYSONISALAWYER	Play as Ken Rosenberg
LOOKLIKELANCE	Play as Lance Vance
WELOVEOURDICK	Play as Love Fist character (Dick)
ROCKANDROLLMAN	Play as Love Fist character (Jezz Torent)
FOXYLITTLETHING	Play as Mercedes
ONEARMEDBANDIT	Play as Phil Cassidy

Code	Effect
CHEATSHAVEBEENCRACKED	Play as Ricardo Diaz
IDONTHAVETHEMONEYSONNY	Play as Sonny Forelli
YOUWONTTAKEMEALIVE	Raise Wanted Level
CHASESTAT	Shows Media Level (when 2+ stars)
TRAVELINSTYLE	Spawn a Bloodring Banger
GETTHEREQUICKLY	Spawn a Bloodring Banger #2
BETTERTHANWALKING	Spawn a Caddie
GETTHEREVERYFASTINDEED	Spawn a Hotring Racer
GETTHEREAMAZINGLYFAST	Spawn a Hotring Racer #2
PANZER	Spawn a Rhino
THELASTRIDE	Spawn a Romero's Hearse
GETTHEREFAST	Spawn a Sabre Turbo
RUBBISHCAR	Spawn a Trashmaster
ROCKANDROLLCAR	Spawn Love Fist's Limo
LIFEISPASSINGMEBY	Speed up game clock
LOADSOFLITTLETHINGS	Sportscars have big wheels
CATSANDDOGS	Stormy Weather
ALOVELYDAY	Sunny/Clear Weather

Grand Theft Auto SanAndreas

Plain Text Cheat Codes

Type these codes during gameplay. The set code can be uppercase or lowercase.

Code	Effect
SPEEDFREAK	All Cars Have Nitro
NIGHTPROWLER	Always Midnight
FLYINGFISH	Boats Fly
BUBBLECARS	Cars Float Away When Hit
STATEOFEMERGENCY	Chaos Mode
BLUESUEDESHOES	Elvis is Everywhere
SPEEDITUP	Faster Gameplay
CRAZYTOWN	Funhouse Theme
ONLYHOMIESALLOWED	Gang Members Everywhere
BIFBUZZ	Gangs Control the Streets
ROCKETMAN	Have Jetpack
PROFESSIONALKILLER	Hitman In All Weapon Stats
CJPHONEHOME	Huge Bunny Hop
Stinglikeabee	Hulk power (SUPER PUNCH)
FULLCLIP	Infinite Ammo, No Reload
WHEELSONLYPLEASE	Invisible car
NATURALTALENT	Max All Vehicle Skill Stats

Code	Effect
BUFFMEUP	Max Muscle
WORSHIPME	Max Respect
HELLOLADIES	Max Sex Appeal
KANGAROO	Mega Jump
STINGLIKEABEE	Mega Punch
NINJATOWN	Ninja Theme
Testeducationalskills	No Wanted Level
STICKLIKEGLUE	Perfect Handling
ROCKETMAYHEM	Recruit Anyone (Rockets)
GHOSTTOWN	Reduced Traffic
BRINGITON	Six Star Wanted Level
SLOWITDOWN	Slower Gameplay
OLDSPEEDDEMON	Spawn Devil
ITSALLBULL	Spawn Dozer
OHDUDE	Spawn Hunter
JUMPJET	Spawn Hydra
MONSTERMASH	Spawn Monster
FOURWHEELFUN	Spawn Quad
VROCKPOKEY	Spawn Racecar
WHERESTHEFUNERAL	Spawn Romero
Dirt bikez	spawn sanchez

Code	Effect
CELEBRITYSTATUS	Spawn Stretch
FLYINGTOSTUNT	Spawn Stunt Plane
TRUEGRIME	Spawn Trashmaster
GOODBYECRUELWORLD	Suicide
PLEASANTLYWARM	Sunny Weather
SCOTTISHSUMMER	Thunderstorm
EVERYONEISPOOR	Traffic is Cheap Cars
EVERYONEISRICH	Traffic is Fast Cars
TOODAMNHOT	Very Sunny Weather
PROFESSIONALSKIT	Weapon Set 2, Professional Tools
UZUMYMW	Weapon set3

Random Text Cheat Codes

Type/enter these codes during gameplay. The set code can be uppercase or lowercase.

Code	Effect
MUNASEF	Adrenaline Mode
YLTEICZ	Aggressive Drivers
allcarsgoboom	All Cars Explode
COXEFGU	All Cars Have Nitro
ZEIIVG	All green lights
XJVSNAJ	Always Midnight
CIKGCGX	Beach Party

Code	Effect
IOWDLAC	Black traffic
PAINTITBLACK	Black Traffic
CPKTNWT	Blow Up All Cars
AFSNMSMW	Boats fly
BSXSGGC	Cars Float Away When Hit
RIPAZHA	Cars Fly
ASNAEB	Clear Wanted Level
BMTPWHR	Country Vehicles and Peds, Get Born 2 Truck Outfit
ASBHGRB	Elvis is Everywhere
FOOOXFT	Everyone is armed
YSOHNUL	Faster Clock
PPGWJHT	Faster Gameplay
BTCDBCB	Fat
CFVFGMJ	Foggy Weather
OUIQDMW	Full Weapon Aiming While Driving
PRIEBJ	Funhouse Theme
MROEMZH	Gang Members Everywhere
MROEMZH	Gangs Control the Streets
BAGOWPG	Have a bounty on your head
YECGAA	Have Jetpack
AIYPWZQP	Have Parachute

Code	Effect
HESOYAM	Health, Armor, $250k
NCSGDAG	Hitman In All Weapon Stats
JHJOECW	Huge Bunny Hop
OSRBLHH	Increase Wanted Level Two Stars
WANRLTW	Infinite Ammo, No Reload
CAINEMVHZC	Infinite Health, except for explosions and falls
CVWKXAM	Infinite Oxygen
XICWMD	Invisible car
BAGUVIX	Large Health Boost
QWIOPKB	Max Muscle
OGXSDAG	Max Respect
EHIBXQS	Max Sex Appeal
LFGMHAL	Mega Jump
IAVENJQ	Mega Punch
AEDUWNV	Never Get Hungry
AEZAKMI	Never Wanted
IFIRSTDOZ	Never Wanted
AFPHULTL	Ninja Theme
OFVIAC	Orange Sky 21:00
ALNSFMZO	Overcast Weather
AJLOJYQY	Peds Attack Each Other, Get Golf Club

Code	Effect
BGLUAWML	Peds Attack You With Weapons, Rocket Launcher
PGGOMOY	Perfect Handling
LLQPFBN	Pink traffic
AUIFRVQS	Rainy Weather
SJMAHPE	Recruit Anyone (9mm)
ZSOXFSQ	Recruit Anyone (Rockets)
THGLOJ	Reduced Traffic
IOJUFZN	Riot Mode
CWJXUOC	Sandstorm
LJSPQK	Six Star Wanted Level
KVGYZQK	Skinny
LIYOAAY	Slower Gameplay
BEKKNQV	Slut Magnet
JCNRUAD	Smash n' Boom
CQZIJMB	Spawn Bloodring Banger
RZHSUEW	Spawn Caddy
EEGCYXT	Spawn Dozer
OHDUDE	Spawn Hunter
JUMPJET	Spawn Hydra
AGBDLCID	Spawn Monster
AKJJYGLC	Spawn Quad

Code	Effect
PDNEJOH	Spawn Racecar
VPJTQWV	Spawn Racecar
JQNTDMH	Spawn Rancher
AIWPRTON	Spawn Rhino
AQTBCODX	Spawn Romero
KRIJEBR	Spawn Stretch
URKQSRK	Spawn Stunt Plane
AMOMHRER	Spawn Tanker Truck
UBHYZHQ	Spawn Trashmaster
KGGGDKP	Spawn Vortex Hovercraft
SZCMAWO	Suicide
AFZLLQLL	Sunny Weather
VKYPQCF	Taxis Have Nitrous, L3 Bunny Hop
MGHXYRM	Thunderstorm
BGKGTJH	Traffic is Cheap Cars
FVTMNBZ	Traffic is Country Vehicles
GUSNHDE	Traffic is Fast Cars
ICIKPYH	Very Sunny Weather
LXGIWYL	Weapon Set 1, Thug's Tools
KJKSZPJ	Weapon Set 2, Professional Tools
UZUMYMW	Weapon Set 3, Nutter Tools

Grand Theft Auto: THE LOST AND DAMNED

Spawn Vehicles

Bring out your cell phone and input the following phone numbers.

Code	Effect
227-555-0142	Spawn a Cognoscenti
227-555-0175	Spawn a Comet
227-555-0100	Spawn a FIB Buffalo
938-555-0100	Spawn a Jetmax
625-555-0150	Spawn a Sanchez
227-555-0147	Spawn a Turismo
625-555-0100	Spawn an NRG-900
359-555-0100	Spawn Annihilator
826-555-0150	Spawn Burrito
245-555-0125	Spawn Double T
245-555-0199	Spawn Hakuchou
245-555-0150	Spawn Hexer
245-555-0100	Spawn Innovation
826-555-0100	Spawn Slamvan

Grand Theft Auto THE BALLAD OF GAY TONY

Cheat Codes

Dial these codes into your cell phone during game play.

Code	Effect
625-555-0200	Akuma (Bike)
272-555-8265	APC(Tank)
359-555-2899	Buzzard(Helicopter)
468-555-0100	Change Weather
938-555-0150	Floater(Boat)
362-555-0100	Health & Armour
482-555-0100	Health, Armor and Advanced Weapons
359-555-7272	Parachute
267-555-0150	Raise Wanted Level
267-555-0100	Remove Wanted Level
486-555-2526	Sniper rifle bullets explode
359-555-0100	Spawn Annihilator
227-555-0110	Spawn Buffalo
227-555-9666	Spawn Bullet GT
227-555-0142	Spawn Cognoscenti
227-555-0175	Spawn Comet

Code	Effect
938-555-0100	Spawn Jetmax
625-555-0100	Spawn NRG-900
625-555-0150	Spawn Sanchez
227-555-0107	Spawn Serrano
227-555-0168	Spawn Super GT
227-555-0147	Spawn Turismo
227-555-0100	Spawns a FIB Buffalo
276-555-2666	Super Punch (exploding punches)
625-555-3273	Vader(Bike)
486-555-0100	Weapons (New & advanced)
486-555-0150	Weapons (Poor)

Grand Theft Auto 4

Cell Phone Passwords

At any time during the game, pull out Niko's phone and dial these numbers for the desired effect.

Please note that cheats will affect missions and achievements.

Password	Effect
468-555-0100	Change weather
486-555-0150	Get a different selection of weapons
486-555-0100	Get a selection of weapons
267-555-0150	Raise wanted level
267-555-0100	Remove wanted level
362-555-0100	Restore armour
482-555-0100	Restore health, armor, and ammo
948-555-0100	Song information
227-555-0142	Spawn a Cognoscenti
227-555-0175	Spawn a Comet
938-555-0100	Spawn a Jetmax
625-555-0150	Spawn a Sanchez
227-555-0168	Spawn a SuperGT
227-555-0147	Spawn a Turismo
359-555-0100	Spawn an Annihiliator
227-555-0100	Spawn an FIB Buffalo
625-555-0100	Spawn an NRG-900

Grand Theft Auto Episodes From Liberty City

Cheat Codes

Dial these codes into your cell phone during game play.

Code	Effect
625-555-0200	Akuma (Bike)
272-555-8265	APC(Tank)
359-555-2899	Buzzard(Helicopter)
468-555-0100	Change Weather
938-555-0150	Floater(Boat)
362-555-0100	Health & Armour
482-555-0100	Health, Armor and Advanced Weapons
359-555-7272	Parachute
267-555-0150	Raise Wanted Level
267-555-0100	Remove Wanted Level
486-555-2526	Sniper rifle bullets explode
359-555-0100	Spawn Annihilator
227-555-0110	Spawn Buffalo
227-555-9666	Spawn Bullet GT
227-555-0142	Spawn Cognoscenti
227-555-0175	Spawn Comet

Code	Effect
938-555-0100	Spawn Jetmax
625-555-0100	Spawn NRG-900
625-555-0150	Spawn Sanchez
227-555-0107	Spawn Serrano
227-555-0168	Spawn Super GT
227-555-0147	Spawn Turismo
227-555-0100	Spawns a FIB Buffalo
276-555-2666	Super Punch (exploding punches)
625-555-3273	Vader(Bike)
486-555-0100	Weapons (New & advanced)
486-555-0150	Weapons (Poor)

Grand Theft Auto 5

Cheats

Press left ctrl + ~ to bring up the cheat menu and bring up phone to enter phone # cheat codes. These will disable achievements.

Code	Effect
346-555-0126	Abigail
346-555-0109	Al
346-555-0118	Amanda
Y, RT, Left, LB, A, Right, Y, Down, X, LB, LB, LB	Ammo
273-555-0117	Answering Mahcine #1
611-555-0152	Answering Mahcine #2
328-555-0122	Answering Mahcine #3
346-555-0160	Answering Mahcine #4
611-555-0160	Answering Mahcine #5
611-555-0179	Answering Mahcine #6
328-555-0142	Answering Mahcine #7
328-555-0153	Answering Mahcine #8
346-555-0176	Blimp
BANDIT	BMX
273-555-0185	Brucie
611-555-0100	Busy Signals #1
611-555-0104	Busy Signals #2

Code	Effect
611-555-0107	Busy Signals #3
611-555-0111	Busy Signals #4
BUZZOFF	Buzzard Attack Helicopter
MAKEITRAIN	Change Weather
611-555-0163	Chasity
328-555-0167	Cheetah
328-555-0167	Chettah (Car)
346-555-0174	Cletus
COMET	Comet
273-555-0132	Dave
328-555-0182	Devon Weston
323-555-5555	Downtown Cab Co.
LIQUOR	Drunk Mode
1-999-3328-4227 (DEATHCAR)	Duke O Death (Must Unlock It in Game)
611-555-0146	Edgar
HIGHEX	Explosive Ammo
HOTHANDS	Explosive Melee Attack
CATCHME	Fast Run
Left, Left, LB, Right, Right, RT, Left, LT, Right	Fast Swim (Gamepad Required)
273-555-0164	Feminine Sexual Art Centre
328-555-0145	First Lieutenant Kyle P. Slater

Code	Effect
328-555-0156	Franklin
SKYFALL	Free Fall (Launches You From The Clouds Point Downward To Avoid Death)
346-555-0134	Friedlander
346-555-0186	Fufu
611-555-0195	Funny Prank Call Response
Y, RT, Left, LB, A, Right, Y, Down, X, LB, LB, LB	Give Guns & Ammo (Gamepad Required)
SKYDIVE	Give Parachute
611-555-0184	Infernus
PAINKILLER	Invincibility (5 Minutes)
346-555-0190 and 273-555-0143	Jimmy
346-555-0148	Jimmy Boston
611-555-0128	Joe
611-555-0169	Josh Bernstein
328-555-0193	Just Music
346-555-0141	Lamar
346-555-0102	Lester
VINEWOOD	Limo
611-555-0126	Liz
LAWYERUP	Lower Wanted Level
611-555-0198	Mailbox Is Full Message

Code	Effect
611-555-0181	Marnie
346-555-0188	Martin Madrazo
328-555-0185	Maude
TURTLE	Max Health + Armor (Also repairs vehicles.)
273-555-0120	Meeryweather
FLOATER	Moon Gravity
346-555-0192	Mysterious Message
346-555-0111	Nigel
346-555-0183	Nikki
273-555-0158	No longer in service message
328-555-0119 & 346-555-0155	Old School Internet Modem Sounds
346-555-0162	Omega
273-555-0125	Oscar
328-555-0110	Patricia Madrazo
ROCKET	PCJ-600 Motorcycle
273-555-0189	Peach
FUGITIVE	Raise Wanted Level
RAPIDGT	Rapid GT
POWERUP	Recharge Ability
611-555-0140	Rickie
328-555-0198	Ron

Code	Effect
OFFROAD	Sanchez Dirt Bike
328-555-0177	Sapphire
611-555-0120	Simeon
SNOWDAY	Slippery Cars
SLOWMO	Slow Motion (Enter 3 Times For Full Effect)
DEADEYE	Slow Motion Aim
328-555-0123	Soloman Richard
1-999-398-4628 (EXTINCT)	Spawn Dodo Plane (Must Unlock It In Game)
1-999-282-2537 (BUBBLES)	Spawn Monkey Blista (Must Unlock It In Game)
328-555-0150	Steve Haines
346-555-0122	Strech
BARNSTORM	Stunt Plane
328-555-0180	Tanisha Jackson
611-555-0191	Tennis Coach
611-555-0199	Tonya
273-555-0168 and 273-555-0197	Tracey
TRASHED	Trashmaster
273-555-0136	Trevor
273-555-0155	Truthseeker

PSP

Grand Theft Auto: Liberty City Stories

Codes

Enter these during gameplay

Code	Effect
UP, UP, UP, SQUARE, SQUARE, TRIANGLE, R1, L1	2 Gangs+14 Characters (Multiplayer)
UP, UP, UP, CIRCLE, CIRCLE, X, L1, R1	4 Gangs+28 Characters (Multiplayer)
UP, UP, UP, X, X, SQUARE, R1, L1	7 Gangs+43 Characters (Multiplayrer)
SQUARE, SQUARE, R1, X, X, L1, CIRCLE, CIRCLE	Aggressive Drivers
TRIANGLE, TRIANGLE, R1, SQUARE, SQUARE, L1, X, X	All Green Lights
TRIANGLE, R1, L1, DOWN, DOWN, R1, R1, TRIANGLE	All Vehicles Chrome Plated
CIRCLE, CIRCLE, R1, TRIANGLE, TRIANGLE, L1, SQUARE, SQUARE	Black Cars
DOWN, DOWN, DOWN, CIRCLE, CIRCLE, X, L1, R1	Bobble Head World
X, Square, Down, X, Square, Up, R1, R1	Calls closest Ped to come hop on/in your vehicle.
CIRCLE, X, DOWN, CIRCLE, X, UP, L1, L1	Cars Drive On Water
CIRCLE, RIGHT, X, UP, RIGHT, X, L1, SQUARE	Change Bike Tire Size
UP, DOWN, CIRCLE, UP, DOWN, SQUARE, L1, R1	Clear Weather

Code	Effect
L1, DOWN, LEFT, R1, X, CIRCLE, UP, TRIANGLE	Commit Suicide
L1, L1, LEFT, L1, L1, RIGHT, X, SQUARE	Destroy All Cars
L1, R1, L1, R1, UP, DOWN, L1, R1	Display Game Credits
L1, L1, LEFT, L1, L1, RIGHT, CIRCLE, X	Faster Clock
R1, R1, L1, R1, R1, L1, DOWN, X	Faster Gameplay
UP, DOWN, TRIANGLE, UP, DOWN, X, L1, R1	Foggy Weather
L1, R1, CIRCLE, L1, R1, X, L1, R1	Full Armor (Blue Bar)
L1, R1, X, L1, R1, SQUARE, L1, R1	Full Health (Red Bar)
DOWN, DOWN, DOWN, TRIANGLE, TRIANGLE, CIRCLE, L1, R1	Have People Follow You
L1, R1, TRIANGLE, L1, R1, CIRCLE, L1, R1	Money Cheat ($250,000)
L1, L1, TRIANGLE, R1, R1, X, SQUARE, CIRCLE	Never Wanted
UP, DOWN, X, UP, DOWN, TRIANGLE, L1, R1	Overcast Weather
L1, L1, R1, L1, L1, R1, UP, TRIANGLE	Peds Attack You
R1, R1, L1, R1, R1, L1, RIGHT, CIRCLE	Peds Have Weapons
L1, L1, R1, L1, L1, R1, LEFT, SQUARE	Peds Riot
L1, UP, LEFT, R1, TRIANGLE, CIRCLE, DOWN, X	Perfect Traction
UP, DOWN, SQUARE, UP, DOWN, CIRCLE, L1, R1	Rainy Weather
L1, UP, RIGHT, R1, TRIANGLE, SQUARE, DOWN, X	Raise Media Attention
L1, R1, SQUARE, L1, R1, TRIANGLE, L1, R1	Raise Wanted Level
L1, L1, LEFT, L1, L1, RIGHT, SQUARE, TRIANGLE	Random Ped Outfit
R1, TRIANGLE, X, R1, SQUARE, CIRCLE, LEFT, RIGHT	Slower Gameplay

Code	Effect
L1, L1, LEFT, L1, L1, RIGHT, TRIANGLE, CIRCLE	Spawn Rhino
TRIANGLE, CIRCLE, DOWN, TRIANGLE, CIRCLE, UP, L1, L1	Spawn Trashmaster
L1, L1, CIRCLE, R1, R1, SQUARE, TRIANGLE, X	Sunny Weather
UP, UP, UP, TRIANGLE, TRIANGLE, CIRCLE, L1, R1	Unlock multiplayer skins
DOWN, DOWN, DOWN, X, X, SQUARE, R1, L1	Upside Down Gameplay
X, X, X, DOWN, DOWN, RIGHT, L1, R1	Upside Down Gameplay2
Triangle, Triangle, Triangle, Up, Up, Right, L, R	Upside Up
UP, SQUARE, SQUARE, DOWN, LEFT, SQUARE, SQUARE, RIGHT	Weapon set 1
UP, CIRCLE, CIRCLE, DOWN, LEFT, CIRCLE, CIRCLE, RIGHT	Weapon set 2
UP, X, X, DOWN, LEFT, X, X, RIGHT	Weapon set 3
X, X, R1, CIRCLE, CIRCLE, L1, TRIANGLE, TRIANGLE	White Cars

Grand Theft Auto: Vice City Stories

Codes

Enter These During Gameplay

Code	Effect
UP, UP, UP, TRIANGLE, TRIANGLE, CIRCLE, L, R	100% of MP Content
UP, UP, UP, SQUARE, SQUARE, TRIANGLE, R, L	25% of MP Content
UP, UP, UP, CIRCLE, CIRCLE, X, L, R	50% of MP Content
UP, UP, UP, X, X, SQUARE, R, L	75% of MP Content
L1, R1, L1, R1, LEFT, CIRCLE, UP, X	All Cars are Black
UP, DOWN, LEFT, RIGHT, SQUARE, SQUARE, L1, R1	Armor
UP, UP, RIGHT, LEFT, TRIANGLE, CIRCLE, CIRCLE, SQUARE	Cars avoid you
RIGHT, UP, LEFT, DOWN, TRIANGLE, TRIANGLE, L1, R1	Chrome Cars
LEFT, DOWN, R1, L1, RIGHT, UP, LEFT, X	Clear Weather
RIGHT, RIGHT, CIRCLE, CIRCLE, L1, R1, DOWN, X	Commit Suicide
L1, R1, R1, LEFT, RIGHT, SQUARE, DOWN, R1	Destroy All Cars
R1, L1, L1, DOWN, UP, X, DOWN, L1	Faster Clock
LEFT, LEFT, R1, R1, UP, TRIANGLE, DOWN, X	Faster Gameplay
LEFT, DOWN, TRIANGLE, X, RIGHT, UP, LEFT, L1	Foggy Weather
UP, DOWN, LEFT, RIGHT, X, X, L1, R1	Get $250000
RIGHT, L1, DOWN, L1, CIRCLE, UP, L1, SQUARE	Guys Follow You
UP, DOWN, LEFT, RIGHT, CIRCLE, CIRCLE, L1, R1	Health
UP, RIGHT, TRIANGLE, TRIANGLE, DOWN, LEFT, X, X	LOWER WANTED LEVEL

Code	Effect
DOWN, UP, RIGHT, L1, L1, SQUARE, UP, L1	Nearest Ped Gets in Your Vehicle (Only works when inside of vehicle)
LEFT, DOWN, L1, R1, RIGHT, UP, LEFT, SQUARE	Overcast Weather
DOWN, TRIANGLE, UP, X, L1, R1, L1, R1	Peds Attack You
UP, L1, DOWN, R1, LEFT, CIRCLE, RIGHT, TRIANGLE	Peds Have Weapons
UP, L1, DOWN, R1, LEFT, CIRCLE, RIGHT, TRIANGLE	Peds Have Weapons
R1, L1, L1, DOWN, LEFT, CIRCLE, DOWN, L1	Peds Riot
DOWN, LEFT, UP, L1, R1, TRIANGLE, CIRCLE, X	Perfect Traction (Press down to 'jump' in cars)
LEFT, DOWN, L1, R1, RIGHT, UP, LEFT, TRIANGLE	Rainy Weather
UP, RIGHT, SQUARE, SQUARE, DOWN, LEFT, CIRCLE, CIRCLE	Raise Wanted Level
LEFT, LEFT, CIRCLE, CIRCLE, DOWN, UP, TRIANGLE, X	Slower Gameplay
UP, L1, DOWN, R1, LEFT, L1, RIGHT, R1	Spawn Rhino
DOWN, UP, RIGHT, TRIANGLE, L1, TRIANGLE, L1, TRIANGLE	Spawn Trashmaster
LEFT, DOWN, R1, L1, RIGHT, UP, LEFT, CIRCLE	Sunny Weather
SQUARE, SQUARE, SQUARE, L1, L1, R1, LEFT, RIGHT	Upside Down Mode 1
LEFT, LEFT, LEFT, R1, R1, L1, RIGHT, LEFT	Upside Down Mode 2
LEFT, RIGHT, X, UP, DOWN, SQUARE, LEFT, RIGHT	Weapon Set 1
LEFT, RIGHT, SQUARE, UP, DOWN, TRIANGLE, LEFT, RIGHT	Weapon Set 2
LEFT, RIGHT, TRIANGLE, UP, DOWN, CIRCLE, LEFT, RIGHT	Weapon Set 3

Grand Theft Auto: Chinatown Wars

Cheats

While playing games enter the cheats below (disables Autosave)

Code	Effect
L1, L1, R1, X, X, CIRCLE, CIRCLE, R1	Armour
Up,Down,Left,Right,Triangle,Square,L1,R1	Cloudy Weather
R1, Triangel, Triangle, Square, Square, R, L1, L1	Decrease Wanted
L1, R1, Triangle, Square, O, X, Up, Down	Explosive Eagle
Up, Down, Left, Right, X, Triangle, L1, R1	Extra Sunny Weather
Down, Left, Right, Square, X, R1, L1	Foggy Weather
L1 L1 >L1 L1<R1 R1	Health
Up,Down,Left,Right,X,Square,R1,L1	Hurricane
L1, L1, R1, Square,Square, Triangle, Triangle, R1	Increase Wanted
Up,Down,Left,Right,O,Triangle,R1,L1	Lots of Rain
Up,Down,Left,Right,Square,O,L1,R1	Rainy Weather
Up,Down,Left,Right,O,X,L1,R1	Sunny Weather
R1, Up, X, Down, Left, R1, X, Right	Weapon Tier 1
R1, Up, CIRCLE, Down, Left, R1, CIRCLE, Right	Weapon Tier 2
R1, Up, TRIANGLE, Down, Left, R1, TRIANGLE, Right	Weapon Tier 4
R1, Up, SQUARE, Down, Left, R1, SQUARE, Right	Weapoon Tier 3

PSOne

Grand Theft Auto

PASSWORDS

Misc. Cheats

Enter the following codes at the Name Entry screen:

Password	Effect
WEYHEY	9,999,990 points
SATANLIVES	99 lives
TVMAN	Access San Andreas parts 1 and 2
T H E S H I T	All Cheats
Caprice	All Cities
TURF	All Cities
URGE	All Cities parts 1 and 2 except Vice City.
BSTARD	All cities, infinite weapons and 99 lives
Groovy	All Weapons
MADEMAN	All Weapons
PECKINPAH	All Weapons, Armor and a Jail Card
BLOWME	Enable Coordinates
EXCREMENT	Five Times Multiplier
HANGTHEDJ	God Cheat
SKYBABIES	Level Select

Password	Effect
INGLORIOUS	Level Select with Extra Options
FECK	Liberty City parts 1 and 2
CHUFF	No Police
EATTHIS	Wanted Level Max ($)

Grand Theft Auto: London 1969

PASSWORDS

Misc. Cheats

Enter the following at the Name Entry screen:

Password	Effect
SIDEBURN	5x Multiplier
BIGBEN	9,999,990 Points
MCVICAR	99 Lives
HAROLDHAND	All Cheats
Razzle	All Levels
READERWIFE	All Levels
FREEMANS	All levels, all weapons, infinite ammunition, Get Out Of Jail Free card, armor, 5X multiplier
GETCARTER	All levels, all weapons, infinite ammunition, Get out of jail free card, armor, 99 lives, 5X multiplier, maximum wanted level, display co-ordinates
SORTED	All levels, and all weapons and unlimited ammunition
DONTMESS	All Weapons and a Jail Card
TOOLEDUP	Infinite Weapons, Armor and a Get Out of Jail Free card.
MAYFAIR	London levels 1-2
PENTHOUSE	London levels 1-3
OLDBILL	Maximum Wanted Level
GRASS	No Cops
SWEENEY	Show Coordinates

Grand Theft Auto 2

CODES

WUGGLES Cheat

First, enter WUGGLES as your player name. Then, on a controller plugged in to port 2 press the following buttons for the desired effects:

Code	Effect
Square Button	$100,000
R-buttons and L-buttons	Change popularity with gangs.
Circle Button	Make police disappear when in pursuit.
Select Button	Toggle Coordinates

PASSWORDS

Misc. Cheats

From the main menu, access Play and then Player Name. Enter your name as any of the following:

Password	Effect
MUCHCASH	$500,000
BIGSCORE	10,000,000 Points
HIGHFIVE	5x Multiplier
NAVARONE	All Weapons
NOFRILLS	Debug Scripts
DESIRES	Get Max Wanted Level
ITSALLUP	Level Select

Password	Effect
DESIRES	Most Wanted
LOSEFEDS	No Police
WUGGLES	Show the area numbers
IGNITION	Turbo Car
LIVELONG	Unlimited Energy
IAMPLAYA	Unlimited Money

PS2

Grand Theft Auto 3

CODES

Button Codes

For these codes to work, enter them during normal gameplay, whilst in any city. (Note: The speed up and slow down codes can be used multiple times to make the game even slower or faster.)

Code	Effect
R2, R2, L1, R2, Left, Down, Right, Up, Left, Down, Right, Up	All Weapons
L2, R2, L1, R1, L2, R2, Triangle, Square, Circle, Triangle, L2, L1	Blow Up Car
L1, L2, R1, R2, R2, R1, L2, Triangle	Clear Weather
L1, L2, R1, R2, R2, R1, L2, Square	Cloudy Weather
R2, R1, Triangle, X, L2, L1, Up, Down	Crazy Pedestrians
Circle, Circle, Circle, Square, Square, Square, Square, Square, L1, Triangle, Circle, Triangle	Faster Time
Right, R2, Circle, R1, L2, Down, L1, R1	Flying Cars
L1, L2, R1, R2, R2, R1, L2, X	Fog Weather
R2, R2, L1, L2, Left, Down, Right, Up, Left, Down, Right, Up	Full Armor
R2, R2, L1, R1, Left, Down, Right, Up, Left, Down, Right, Up	Full Heath
Circle, Circle, Circle, Circle, Circle, Circle, R1, L2, L1, Triangle, Circle, Triangle	Get A Tank
R1, L1, R2, L1, Left, R1, R1, Triangle	Great Handling In Car (Press L3 to jump!)

Code	Effect
R2, R2, L1, R2, Left, Right, Left, Right, Left, Right	Higher Wanted Level
R2, R2, L1, L1, Left, Down, Right, Up, Left, Down, Right, Up	Lots of Money
R2, R2, L1, R2, Up, Down, Up, Down, Up, Down	Lower Wanted Level
L1, L1, Square, R2, Triangle, L1, Triangle	Make Cars Invisible
Square, L1, Circle, Down, L1, R1, Triangle, Right, L1, X	More Gore blow off limbs and head (no confirmation message)
Down, Up, Left, Up, X, R1, R2, L1, L2	Pedestrians All Hate You
Down, Up, Left, Up, X, R1, R2, L2, L1	Pedestrians Fight Each Other
L1, L2, R1, R2, R2, R1, L2, Circle	Rainy Weather
Triangle, Up, Right, Down, Square, R1, R2	Slow Down Gameplay
Triangle, Up, Right, Down, Square, L1, L2	Speed Up Gameplay
Right, Down, Left, Up, L1, L2, Up, Left, Down, Right	Wear Any Outfit

Grand Theft Auto Vice City

CODES

Cheat Codes

Enter these codes during gameplay without pausing:

Code	Effect
Right, R1, Up, L2, L2, Left, R1 ,L1, R1, R1	All Traffic lights will remain green.
Triangle, L1, Triangle, R2, Square, L1, L1	All Vehicles Invisible (except motorcycles)
R1, R2, L1, R2, L, D, R, U, L, D, R, U	All Weapons #1
R1, R2, L1, R2, L, D, R, U, L, D, D, L	All Weapons #2
R1, R2, L1, R2, L, D, R, U, L, D, D, D	All Weapons #3
R1, R2, L1, X, Left, Down, Right, Up, Left, Down, Right, Up	Armor Code
O, L2, U, R1, L, X, R1, L1, L, O	Black Cars
R2, L2, R1, L1, L2, R2, S, T, O, T, L2, L1	Blow Up Cars
R, R, L, U, L1, L2, L, U, D, R	Change Clothes
Right,L1,Circle,L2,Left,X,R1,L1,L1,X	Chicks with Guns
R2, X, L1, L1, L2, L2, L2, T	Cloudy Weather
R, L2, D, R1, L, L, R1, L1, L2, L1	Commit Suicide
O, L1, D, L2, L, X, R1, L1, R, X	Fake Code (doesn't do anything)
Circle,X,L1,L1,R2,X,X,Circle,Triangle	Fanny Magnet (Girls follow Tommy)
Triangle, Up, Right, Down, L2, L1, Square	Fast Motion
Right, R2, O, R1, L2, Down, L1, R1	Flying Cars

Code	Effect
R2, X, L1, L1, L2, L2, L2, X	Foggy Weather
R, L1, O, L2, L, X, R1, L1, L1, X	Gals Drop Weapons
R1, R2, L1, O, Left, Down, Right, Up, Left, Down, Right, Up	Health Code
R2, Circle, Up, L1, Right, R1, Right, Up, Square, Triangle	Hovering Boats
Right, R2, Circle, R1, L2, Square, R1, R2	Hovering Cars
R1, R1, O, R2, U, D, U, D, U, D	Lower Wanted Level
R2,Circle,R1,L2,Left,R1,L1,R2,L2	Mad Cars
R2, O, U, L1, R, R1, R, U, S, T	Media Level Meter
D, U, U, U, X, R2, R1, L2, L2	Pedestrian Attack (cannot be turned off)
D, L, U, L, X, R2, R1, L2, L1	Pedestrian Riot (cannot be turned off)
R2, R1, X, T, X, T, U, D	Pedestrians have weapons
T, R1, R1, L, R1, L1, R2, L1	Perfect Handling
Circle,L1,Down,L2,Left,X,R1,L1,Right,Circle	Pink Cars
O, R2, D, R1, L, R, R1, L1, X, L2	Play As Candy Suxxx
R1, O, R2, L1, R, R1, L1, X, R2	Play As Hilary King
R, L1, U, L2, L1, R, R1, L1, X, R1	Play As Ken Rosenberg
O, L2, L, X, R1, L1, X, L1	Play As Lance Vance
D, L1, D, L2, L, X, R1, L1, X, X	Play As Love Fist Guy #1
R1, L2, R2, L1, R, R2, L, X, S, L1	Play As Love Fist Guy #2
R2, L1, U, L1, R, R1, R, U, O, T	Play As Mercedes

Code	Effect
R, R1, U, R2, L1, R, R1, L1 ,R, O	Play As Phil Cassady
L1, L2, R1, R2, D, L1, R2, L2	Play As Ricardo Diaz
O, L1, O, L2, L, X, R1, L1, X, X	Play As Sonny Forelli
R1, R1, O, R2, L, R, L, R, L, R	Raise Wanted Level
Triangle, Up, Right, Down, Square, R2, R1	Slow Motion
U, R, R, L1, R, U, S, L2	Spawn A Bloodring Banger
D, R1, O, L2, L2, X, R1, L1, L, L	Spawn A Bloodring Racer
O, L1, U, R1, L2, X, R1, L1, O, X	Spawn A Caddie
R1, O, R2, R, L1, L2, X, X, S, R1	Spawn A Hotring Racer #1
R2, L1, O, R, L1, R1, R, U, O, R2	Spawn A Hotring Racer #2
R2,Up,L2,Left,Left,R1,L1,Circle,Right	Spawn A Love Fist Limo
O, O, L1, O, O, O, L1, L2, R1, T, O, T	Spawn A Rhino
D, R2, D, R1, L2, L, R1, L1, L, R	Spawn A Romero's Hearse
R, L2, D, L2, L2, X, R1, L1, O, L	Spawn A Sabre Turbo
O, R1, O, R1, L, L, R1, L1, O, R	Spawn A Trashmaster
R2, L1, circle, right, L1, R1, right, up, circle, R2	Spawns the Hot Ring Racer
O, O, L1, S, L1, S, S, S, L1, T, O, T	Speed Up Time
R2, X, L1, L1, L2, L2, L2, O	Stormy Weather
R2,X,L1,L1,L2,L2,L2,Triangle	Sunny Weather
R2, X, L1, L1, L2, L2, L2, S	Very Cloudy Weather
R1, X, Triangle, Right, R2, Square, Up, Down, Square	Weird Wheels

Grand Theft Auto SanAndreas

CODES

Cheat Codes

Enter these during gameplay without pausing:

Code	Effect
R1, R2, L1 , X, Left , Down, Right, Up, Left, Down, Right, Up	$250,000, full health and armor (also repairs cars if you are in one)
RIGHT, R2, UP, UP, R2, CIRCLE, SQUARE, R2, L1, RIGHT, DOWN, L1	Aggressive Drivers
R2, Circle, R1, L2, Left R1, L1, R2, L2	Aggressive Traffic
LEFT, TRIANGLE, R1, L1, UP, SQUARE, TRIANGLE, DOWN, CIRCLE, L2, L1, L1	All Cars Nos
L1, Circle, Triangle, L1, L1, Square, L2, Up, Down, Left	All Pedestrians Are Elvis
up,x,triangle,x,triangle,x,square,R2,right	all taxis get nitro + jump up when you press L3
L2, RIGHT, L1, UP, X, L1, L2, R2, R1, L1, L1, L1	All Traffic is Junk Cars
Right, R1, Up, L2, L2, Left, R1, L1, R1, R1	All Traffic Lights Stay Green
Triangle, L1, Triangle, R2, Square, L1, L1	All Vehicles Invisible (Except Motorcycles)
SQUARE, L1, R1, RIGHT, X, UP, L1, LEFT, LEFT	always midnight (time stuck at 00:00)
x,x,square,r1,l1,x,down,left,x	andrenaline mode
L1, L2, L2, Up, Down, Down, Up, R1, R2, R2	Any vehicle you punch this in, can blow up anything like a tank.
SQUARE, RIGHT, SQUARE, SQUARE, L2, X, TRIANGLE, X, TRIANGLE	Attracts Prostitutes with Sex Toys/Gimp Suit
Circle, L2, Up, R1, Left, X, R1, L1, Left, Circle	Black Traffic

Code	Effect
X, Square, Down, X, Square, Up, R1, R1	Calls the nearest ped to get in your car or get on your bike. Only gives a confirmation message if you're in a vehicle and there's a ped nearby.
Square, R2, Down, Down, Left, Down, Left, Left, L2, X	Cars Float Away When Hit
square, down, L2, up, L1, circle, up, x, left	Cars Fly
Right, R2, Circle, R1, L2, Square, R1, R2	Cars on Water
L2, RIGHT, L1, TRIANGLE, RIGHT, RIGHT, R1, L1, RIGHT, L1, L1, L1	Chaos mode
Triangle, Triangle, L1, Square, Square, Circle, Square, Down, Circle	Civilians are fast food workers & clowns, CJ is a clown, cars are pizza scooter, BF Injection, HotKnife, Tug, Quad, etc.
Right, L2, Down, R1, Left, Left, R1, L1, L2, L1	Commit Suicide
R2, L2, R1, L1, L2, R2, Square, Triangle, Circle, Triangle, L2, L1	Destroy Cars
Up, Up, Down, Down, Square, Circle, L1, R1, Triangle, Down.	Everyone bikini babes, all cars beach cars, Cj in shorts and flipflops.
Circle, Circle, L1, Square, L1, Square, Square, Square, L1, Triangle, O, Triangle	Faster Clock
Triangle, Up, Right, Down, L2, L1, Square	Faster Gameplay
R2, Circle, Up, L1, Right, R1, Right, Up, Square, Triangle	Flying Boats
R2, X, L1, L1, L2, L2, L2, X	Fog
up, up, square, L2, right, x, R1, down, R2, circle	Full Weapon Aiming Whilst Driving
Left, Right, Right, Right, Left, X, Down, Up, Square, Right	Gang members spawn much faster
Circle, Right, Circle, Right, Left, Square, X Down	Gives you an automatic six star wanted level

Code	Effect
DOWN, SQUARE, X, LEFT, R1, R2, LEFT, DOWN, DOWN, L1, L1, L1	Hitman In all weapon
square,square,R2,left,up,square,R2,X,X,X	Improve Suspension
up, L1, R1, up, right, up, x, L2, x, L1	Increase car speed
L1, R1, SQUARE, R1, LEFT, R2, R1, LEFT, SQUARE, DOWN, L1, L1	Inf Ammo
Down, X, Right, Left, Right, R1, Right, Down, Up, Triangle	Infinite health, still hurt from explosions, drowning, and falling.
Down, Left, L1, Down, Down, R2, Down, L2, Down	Infinite Lung Capacity
Triangle, R1, R1, Left, R1, L1, R2, L1	Insane Handling
Left, Right, L1, L2, R1, R2, Up, Down, Left, Right	Jetpack
Up, Up, Triangle, Triangle, Up, Up, Left, Right, Square, R2, R2	Jump 10 times higher
Triangle, Square, Circle, Circle, Square, Circle, Circle, L1, L2, L2, R1, R2.	Jump 100 feet in air on bike
CIRCLE, RIGHT, CIRCLE, RIGHT, LEFT, SQUARE, TRIANGLE, UP	Locks wanted level at however many stars you have. They will NEVER increase or decrease, not even with bribes/cheats. Still get attacked in impound.
R1, R1, Circle, R2, Up, Down, Up, Down, Up, Down	Lower Wanted Level
SQUARE, L2, X, R1, L2, L2, LEFT, R1, RIGHT, L1, L1, L1	Max All Vehicle stats (Driving, Flying Bike, Cycling)
Triangle, Up ,Up, Left, Right, Square, Circle, Down	Max Fat
triangle,up,up,left,right,square,circle,left	Max Muscle
L1, R1, TRIANGLE, DOWN, R2, X, L1, UP, L2, L2, L1, L1	Max Respect

Code	Effect
CIRCLE, TRIANGLE, TRIANGLE, UP, CIRCLE, R1, L2, UP, TRIANGLE, L1, L1, L1	Max Sex appeal
R2, X, L1, L1, L2, L2, L2, Square	Morning
SQUARE, L2, R1, TRIANGLE, UP, SQUARE, L2, UP, X	Never become hungry
R2, X, L1, L1, L2, L2, L2, Triangle	Night
L2, Up, R1, R1, Left, R1, R1, R2, Right, Down	No citizens or cops, only gang members having gun fights
X, Down, Up, R2, Down, Triangle, L1, Triangle, Left	No Peds, Hardly any traffic, Parked cars still spawn
R2, X, L1, L1, L2, L2, L2, Down	Noon
Left, Left, L2, R1, Right, Square, Square, L1, L2, X	Orange Sky
R2, X, L1, L1, L2, L2, L2, Square	Overcast
Down, Up, Up, Up, X, R2, R1, L2, L2	Pedestrian Attack (cannot be turned off)
Down, Left, Up, Left, X, R2, R1, L2, L1	Pedestrian Riot (cannot be turned off)
R2, R1, X, Triangle, X, Triangle, Up, Down	Pedestrians have weapons
X, L1, UP, SQUARE, DOWN, X, L2, TRIANGLE, DOWN, R1, L1, L1	Peds Attack (Guns)
X X Down R2 L2 O R1 O Square	Peds become asian dudes with Katana's. Mostly black cars and motorcycles patrol the streets.
Circle, L1, Down, L2, Left, X, R1, L1, Right, Circle	Pink Traffic
Right, L2, L2, Down, L2, Up, Up, L2, R2	Prostitutes pay you instead of you paying them
R1, R1, Circle, R2, Right, Left, Right, Left, Right, Left	Raise Wanted Level
DOWN, SQUARE, UP, R2, R2, UP, RIGHT, RIGHT, UP	Recruit Anyone (9mm)
R2, R2, R2, X, L2, L1, R2, L1, DOWN, X	Recruits Anyone (w/Rockets)

Code	Effect
Up, Down, L1, L1, L2, L2, L1, L2, R1, R2	Sand Storm
Triangle, Up, Up, Left, Right, Square, Circle, Right	Skinny
Triangle, Up, Right, Down, Square, R2, R1	Slower Gameplay
Right, Up, R1, R1, R1, Down, Triangle, Triangle, X, Circle, L1, L1	Spawn a Monster
Left, Right, L1, L2, R1, R2, R2, Up, Down, Right, L1	spawn a parachute
Circle, Circle, L1, Circle, Circle, Circle, L1, L2, R1, Triangle, Circle, Triangle	Spawn A Rhino
R2, Up, L2, Left, Left, R1, L1, Circle, Right	Spawn a Stretch
Down, R1, Circle, L2, L2, X, R1, L1, Left, Left	Spawn Bloodring Banger
Circle, L1, Up, R1, L2, X, R1, L1, Circle, X	Spawn Caddy
R2, L1, L1, RIGHT, RIGHT, UP, UP, X, L1, LEFT	spawn dozer
Right, R1, Up, L2, L2, Left, R1, L1, R1, R1	Spawn Faster Cars
R1, circle, R2, Right, L1, L2, X (2), Square, R1	Spawn Hotring Racer #1
R2, L1, Circle, Right, L1, R1, Right, Up, circle, R2	Spawn Hotring Racer #2
CIRCLE, X, L1, CIRCLE, CIRCLE, L1, CIRCLE, R1, R2, L2, L1, L1	Spawn Hunter
Up, Right, Right, L1, Right, Up, Square, L2	Spawn Rancher
R1, UP, LEFT, RIGHT, R2, UP, RIGHT, SQUARE, RIGHT, L2, L1, L1	Spawn Tanker
Triangle, Triangle, Square, Circle, X, L1, L1, Down, Up	Spawns Hydra
Left, Left, Down, Down, Up, Up, Square, Circle, Triangle, R1, R2	Spawns Quadbike
Triangle, Triangle, Square, Circle, X, L1, L2, Down,	Spawns Vortex

Code	Effect
Down	
R2, X, L1, L1, L2, L2, L2, Circle	Storm
Circle, Up, L1, L2, Down, R1, L1, L1, Left, Left, X, Triangle.	Stuntplane
Up, Left, X, Triangle, R1, Circle, Circle, Circle, L2	Super Punch
TRIANGLE, LEFT, SQUARE, R2, UP, L2, DOWN, L1, X, L1, L1, L1	Traffic is Country Vehicles
L1 L1 R1 R1 L2 L1 R2 Down Left Up	Turns All Vehicles Into Country Vehicles
Down, R2, Down, R1, L2, Left, R1, L1, Left, Right	Unlock Romero
Circle, R1, Circle, R1, Left, Left, R1, L1, Circle, Right	Unlock Trashmaster
R1, R2, L1, R2, Left, Down, Right, Up, Left, Down, Right, Up	Weapons 1
R1, R2, L1, R2, Left, Down, Right, Up, Left, Down, Down, Left	Weapons 2
R1, R2, L1, R2, Left, Down, Right, Up, Left , Down, Down, Down	Weapons 3
L2, DOWN, DOWN, LEFT, SQUARE, LEFT, R2, SQUARE, X, R1, L1, L1	Weather Cloudy

Grand Theft Auto: Liberty City Stories

CODES

Codes

Enter these during gameplay

Code	Effect
SQUARE, SQUARE, R1, X, X, L1, CIRCLE, CIRCLE	Aggressive Drivers
TRIANGLE, TRIANGLE, R1, SQUARE, SQUARE, L1, X, X	All Green Lights
TRIANGLE, R1, L1, DOWN, DOWN, R1, R1, TRIANGLE	All Vehicles Chrome Plated
CIRCLE, CIRCLE, R1, TRIANGLE, TRIANGLE, L1, SQUARE, SQUARE	Black Cars
DOWN, DOWN, DOWN, CIRCLE, CIRCLE, X, L1, R1	Bobble Head World
X, Square, Down, X, Square, Up, R1, R1	Calls closest Ped to come hop on/in your vehicle.
CIRCLE, X, DOWN, CIRCLE, X, UP, L1, L1	Cars Drive On Water
CIRCLE, RIGHT, X, UP, RIGHT, X, L1, SQUARE	Change Bike Tire Size
UP, DOWN, CIRCLE, UP, DOWN, SQUARE, L1, R1	Clear Weather
L1, DOWN, LEFT, R1, X, CIRCLE, UP, TRIANGLE	Commit Suicide
L1, L1, LEFT, L1, L1, RIGHT, X, SQUARE	Destroy All Cars
L1, R1, L1, R1, UP, DOWN, L1, R1	Display Game Credits
L1, L1, LEFT, L1, L1, RIGHT, CIRCLE, X	Faster Clock
R1, R1, L1, R1, R1, L1, DOWN, X	Faster Gameplay
UP, DOWN, TRIANGLE, UP, DOWN, X, L1, R1	Foggy Weather

Code	Effect
L1, R1, CIRCLE, L1, R1, X, L1, R1	Full Armor (Blue Bar)
L1, R1, X, L1, R1, SQUARE, L1, R1	Full Health (Red Bar)
DOWN, DOWN, DOWN, TRIANGLE, TRIANGLE, CIRCLE, L1, R1	Have People Follow You
L1, R1, TRIANGLE, L1, R1, CIRCLE, L1, R1	Money Cheat ($250,000)
L1, L1, TRIANGLE, R1, R1, X, SQUARE, CIRCLE	Never Wanted
UP, DOWN, X, UP, DOWN, TRIANGLE, L1, R1	Overcast Weather
L1, L1, R1, L1, L1, R1, UP, TRIANGLE	Peds Attack You
R1, R1, L1, R1, R1, L1, RIGHT, CIRCLE	Peds Have Weapons
L1, L1, R1, L1, L1, R1, LEFT, SQUARE	Peds Riot
L1, UP, LEFT, R1, TRIANGLE, CIRCLE, DOWN, X	Perfect Traction
UP, DOWN, SQUARE, UP, DOWN, CIRCLE, L1, R1	Rainy Weather
L1, UP, RIGHT, R1, TRIANGLE, SQUARE, DOWN, X	Raise Media Attention
L1, R1, SQUARE, L1, R1, TRIANGLE, L1, R1	Raise Wanted Level
R1, TRIANGLE, X, R1, SQUARE, CIRCLE, LEFT, RIGHT	Slower Gameplay
L1, L1, LEFT, L1, L1, RIGHT, TRIANGLE, CIRCLE	Spawn Rhino
TRIANGLE, CIRCLE, DOWN, TRIANGLE, CIRCLE, UP, L1, L1	Spawn Trashmaster
L1, L1, CIRCLE, R1, R1, SQUARE, TRIANGLE, X	Sunny Weather
UP, SQUARE, SQUARE, DOWN, LEFT, SQUARE, SQUARE, RIGHT	Weapon set 1
UP, CIRCLE, CIRCLE, DOWN, LEFT, CIRCLE, CIRCLE, RIGHT	Weapon set 2
UP, X, X, DOWN, LEFT, X, X, RIGHT	Weapon set 3
X, X, R1, CIRCLE, CIRCLE, L1, TRIANGLE, TRIANGLE	White Cars

Grand Theft Auto: Vice City Stories

CODES

Enter the Following During Gameplay

Code	Effect
Left, Right, X, Up, Down, Square, Left, Right	Acquire Weapon Set 1
Left, Right, Square, Up, Down, Triangle, Left, Right	Acquire Weapon Set 2
Left, Right, Triangle, Up, Down, Circle, Left, Right	Acquire Weapon Set 3
UP, DOWN, TRIANGLE, X, L1, R1, LEFT, CIRCLE	All Green Lights
Up, Up, Right, Left, Triangle, Circle, Circle, Square	Cars Avoid You
LEFT, DOWN, R1, L1, RIGHT, UP, LEFT, X	Clear Weather
L1, R1, R1, Left, Right, Square, Down, R1	Destroy Cars Near You
LEFT, DOWN, TRIANGLE, X, RIGHT, UP, LEFT, L1	Foggy Weather
Up, Down, Left, Right, Square, Square, L1, R1	Full Armor
Up, Down, Left, Right, Circle, Circle, L1, R1	Full Health
Up, Down, Left, Right, X, X, L1, R1	Gain $250,000
Right, L1, Down, L1, Circle, Up, L1, Square	Guy Magnet
Up, Right, Triangle, Triangle, Down, Left, X, X	Never Wanted (turns off after rampages)
Down, Left, Up, L1, R1, Triangle, Circle, X	No Traction
Left, Down, L1, R1, Right, Up, Left, Square	Overcast Weather
DOWN, TRIANGLE, UP, X, L1, R1, L1, R1	Peds Attack You
UP, L1, DOWN, R1, LEFT, CIRCLE, RIGHT, TRIANGLE	Peds Have Weapons

Code	Effect
R1, L1, L1, DOWN, LEFT, CIRCLE, DOWN, L1	Peds Riot
Left, Down, L1, R1, Right, Up, Left, Triangle	Rainy Weather
Up, Right, Square, Square, Down, Left, Circle, Circle	Raise Wanted Level
DOWN, UP, RIGHT, L1, L1, SQUARE, UP, L1	Ride With Me
Left, Left, Circle, Circle, Down, Up, Triangle, X	Slow Down Game
Up, L1, Down, R1, Left, L1, Right, R1	Spawn Rhino Tank
Down, Up, Right, Triangle, L1, Triangle, L1, Triangle	Spawn Trashmaster Truck
R1, L1, L1, Down, Up, X, Down, L1	Speed Up Clock
Left, Left, R1, R1, Up, Triangle, Down, X	Speed Up Game
LEFT, DOWN, R1, L1, RIGHT, UP, LEFT, CIRCLE	Sunny Weather
L1, R1, L1, R1, Left, Circle, Up, X	Vehicles Color Changed to Black (Except for Cop Cars)
Right, Up, Left, Down, Triangle, Triangle, L1, R1	Vehicles Color Changed to Chrome (Including Cop Cars)
Right, Right, Circle, Circle, L1, R1, Down, X	Wasted! (Commit Suicide)

PS3

Grand Theft Auto SanAndreas

CODES

Grand Theft Auto: San Andreas (PlayStation 3) Cheats Code.

Enter these during gameplay without pausing:

Code	Effect
Triangle, Right, Down, L2, L1, Square, Square, R2, R1	Adrenalin
Square, Left, X, Right, L2, L1, R2, R1, Right, Right, Up	All Car Are Great
X, Triangle, X, Triangle, Square, Up, Up, Down, L2, L1, R2	All Car Are Sh*t
Down, X, Down, X, R2, R1, Up, Triangle, Left, Circle	Ammo
Circle, Square, Square, Circle, Triangle, L2, Up, L1, L1, Down, Down, X	Apache
Right, R1, Circle, R2, L1, Square, R2, R1	Back To The Future
Up, Up, Down, Down, Square, Circle, L2, R2, Triangle, Down	Beach Party
Circle, L1, Up, R2, Left, X, R2, L2, Left, Circle	Black cars
R1, L1, R2, L2, L1, R1, Square, Triangle, Circle, Triangle, L1, L2	Blow Up Cars
Triangle, X, X, Circle, Circle, Square, L2, R1, L1, R2	Bullet Proof
Triangle, Square, Circle, Circle, Square, Circle, Circle, L2, L1, L1, R2, R1	CJ Phone Home
R1, X, L2, L2, L1, L1, L1, Square	Cloudy Weather
Right, Right, Left, Left, Up, Down, Triangle, Triangle, R2, R1, X, X	Country Side Invasion

Code	Effect
X, R1, L1, L2, Down, Square, Left, X, X, Right, R1	Dozer
L1, L1, R1, R1, L2, R2, Down, Down, Up, Up, X, Triangle	Drive By
X, Down, Down, X, Up, Up, L2, R1, R1, L2	Dusk
L2, Circle, Triangle, L2, L2, Square, L1, Up, Down, Left	Elvis Lives
Down, Up, Up, Up, X, R1, R2, L1, L1	Everybody Attacks Player
R1, X, L2, L2, L1, L1, L1, Down	Extra Sunny Weather
Triangle, Up, Right, Down, L1, L2, Square	Fast Time
Circle, Circle, L2, Square, L2, Square, Square, Square, L2, Triangle, Circle, Triangle	Fast Weather
Triangle, Up, Up, Left, Right, Square, Circle, Down	Fat
Triangle, Triangle, Square, Circle, X, L2, L2, Down, Up	Fly Boy
L2, L2, L1, L1, Up, Down, Square, Circle, Square, Square, Triangle	Flying Cars
R1, Circle, Up, L2, Right, R2, Right, Up, Square, Triangle	Flying Fish
R1, X, L2, L2, L1, L1, L1, X	Foggy Weather
Circle, L2, R2, Circle, L2, R2, X, R2, R2, R1, R1	Fun House
Down, Right, R2, L2, Triangle, Square, Square, Circle, Circle	GangLand
L2, L2, R2, R1, Up, L2, Down, L1, Right	Gangs
Circle, L2, Up, R2, L1, X, R2, L2, Circle, X	Golf Cart
Down, R1, Down, R2, L1, Left, R2, L2, Left, Right	Hearse
Up, Up, Triangle, Triangle, Up, Up, Left, Right, Square, R1, R1	High Jump
Left, Right, L2, L1, R2, R1, Up, Down, Left, Right	JetPack

Code	Effect
Right, Left, Triangle, Circle, Circle, R2, R1, R1, R1	Love Conquers All
R1, Up, L1, Left, Left, R2, L2, Circle, Right	Love Fist
R1, Circle, R2, L1, Left, R2, L2, R1, L1	Mad Drivers
Down, Left, Up, Left, X, R1, R2, L1, L2	Mayhem
X, Down, Down, X, Up, Up, L2, L1, L1, L2	Midnight
R2, R1, L2, X, Left, Down, Right, Up, Left, Down, Right, Up	Money Armour Health
Right, Up, R2, R2, R2, Down, Triangle, Triangle, X, Circle, L2, L2	Monster Truck
Triangle, Up, Up Left, Right, Square, Circle, Left	Muscle
Triangle, X, X, X, L2, L1, Left, Left, Up, Up	Ninja
R1, R2, R1, R2, L2, Up, L2, Up, Down, Down, Square	Nitro
Up, Down, Down, Left, Right, L2, L2, L1, R2, R2, R1	No Food
Circle, Right, Circle, Right, Left, Square, Triangle, Up	Not Wanted
Triangle, L2, Triangle, R1, Square, L2, L2	Only Render Wheels
Left, Right, L2, L1, R2, R1, R1, Up, Down, Right, L2	Parachute
Circle, L2, Down, L1, Left, X, R2, L2, Right, Circle	Pink Cars
Square, Triangle, X, Circle, Up, Left, Down, Right, L2, R2	Predator
Left, Left, Down, Down, Up, Up, Square, Circle, Triangle, R2, R1	Quad
R1, X, L2, L2, L1, L1, L1, Circle	Rainy Weather
R2, R1, R1, R2, R1, R1, Left, Left, Right, Right, Left, Left	Recruit Me
R2, R1, R1, R2, R1, R1, Left, Left, Right, Left, Left, Right	Recruit Me AK47

Code	Effect
R2, R1, R1, R2, R1, R1, Left, Left, Right, Right, Right, Left	Recruit Me Rocket
Up, Left, Left, Down, Circle, Square, X, Triangle, Triangle, L2, R2	Respect
Down, Right, Square, Square, Triangle, Triangle, X, X, L2, L1	Riot
Up, Down, L2, L2, L1, L1, L2, L1, R2, R1	Sand Storm
R1, L2, L1, R1, R1, Triangle, R1, X, X, Triangle	Scuba
Up, Left, Left, Down, Circle, Square, Triangle, Triangle, Square, X, R1, R1	Sex Appeal
Triangle, Up, Up, Left, Right, Square, Circle, Right	Skinny
Triangle, Up, Right, Down, Square, R1, R2	Slow Time
Up, Left, Left, Down, Circle, Square, L2, L2, L1, R2, R1	Stamina
Down, R2, Circle, L1, L1, X, R2, L2, Left, Left	Stock Car 1
Up, Right, Right, L2, Right, Up, Square, L1	Stock Car 2
R2, Circle, R1, Right, L2, L1, X, X, Square, R2	Stock Car 3
R1, L2, Circle, Right, L2, R2, Right, Up, Circle, R1	Stock Car 4
R1, Triangle, R1, Triangle, Circle, Circle, Left, Right, Up, Up	Storm
Triangle, R2, R2, Left, R2, L2, R1, L2	Strong Grip
Circle, Up, L2, L1, Down, R2, L2, L2, Left, Left, X, Triangle	Stunt Plane
Right, L1, Down, R2, Left, Left, R2, L2, L1, L2	Suicide
R1, X, L2, L2, L1, L1, L1, Triangle	Sunny Weather
L1, R2, R1, L2, X, X, Circle, Circle, Square, Square	Super Power Car
X, L2, L2, X, Square, Circle, R1, R2, R1, R2	Super Punch
Circle, Circle, L2, Circle, Circle, Circle, L2, L1, R2, Triangle, Circle, Triangle	Tank

Code	Effect
R1, L1, L2, R2, Triangle, Down, Down, X, Left, Square, Circle	Tanker
Right, R2, Up, L1, L1, Left, R2, L2, R2, R2	Traffic Lights
Circle, R2, Circle, R2, Left, Left, R2, L2, Circle, RIGHT	TrashMaster
L2, L1, L1, Up, Down, Down, Up, R2, R1, R1	Vehicle Of Death
Up, Left, Left, Down, Circle, Square, Right, Left, Triangle, Triangle, X	Vehicle Skill
X, X, Triangle, L2, R2, Circle, L2, Circle, Up, Down, R1	Village People
Triangle, Triangle, Square, Circle, X, L2, L1, Down, Down	Vortex
Circle, Right, Circle, Right, Left, Square, X, Down	Wanted
R2, R2, Circle, R1, Up, Down, Up, Down, Up, Down	Wanted Level Down
R2, R2, Circle, R1, Left, Right, Left, Right, Left, Right	Wanted Level Up
R2, L2, X, X, Circle, Square, Triangle, Triangle, L2, R2	WasteLand
R2, R1, L2, R1, Left, Down, Right, Up, Left, Down, Right, Up	Weapon 1
R2, R1, L2, R1, Left, Down, Right, Up, Left, Down, Down, Left	Weapon 2
R2, R1, L2, R1, Left, Down, Right, Up, Left, Down, Down, Down	Weapon 3
R1, R2, X, Triangle, X, Triangle, Up, Down	Weapon For All
Up, Left, Left, Down, Circle, Square, R2, Right, Right, R2, R1	Weapon Skill

Grand Theft Auto: THE LOST AND DAMNED

CODES

Spawn Vehicles

Bring out your cell phone and input the following phone numbers.

Code	Effect
227-555-0142	Spawn a Cognoscenti
227-555-0175	Spawn a Comet
227-555-0100	Spawn a FIB Buffalo
938-555-0100	Spawn a Jetmax
625-555-0150	Spawn a Sanchez
227-555-0147	Spawn a Turismo
625-555-0100	Spawn an NRG-900
359-555-0100	Spawn Annihilator
826-555-0150	Spawn Burrito
245-555-0125	Spawn Double T
245-555-0199	Spawn Hakuchou
245-555-0150	Spawn Hexer
245-555-0100	Spawn Innovation
826-555-0100	Spawn Slamvan

Grand Theft Auto THE BALLAD OF GAY TONY

CODES

Cheat Codes

Dial these codes into your cell phone during game play.

Code	Effect
625-555-0200	Akuma (Bike)
272-555-8265	APC(Tank)
359-555-2899	Buzzard(Helicopter)
468-555-0100	Change Weather
938-555-0150	Floater(Boat)
362-555-0100	Health & Armour
482-555-0100	Health, Armor and Advanced Weapons
359-555-7272	Parachute
267-555-0150	Raise Wanted Level
267-555-0100	Remove Wanted Level
486-555-2526	Sniper rifle bullets explode
359-555-0100	Spawn Annihilator
227-555-9666	Spawn Bullet GT
227-555-0142	Spawn Cognoscenti
227-555-0175	Spawn Comet

Code	Effect
938-555-0100	Spawn Jetmax
625-555-0100	Spawn NRG-900
625-555-0150	Spawn Sanchez
227-555-0168	Spawn Super GT
227-555-0147	Spawn Turismo
227-555-0100	Spawns a FIB Buffalo
276-555-2666	Super Punch (exploding punches)
625-555-3273	Vader(Bike)
486-555-0100	Weapons (New & advanced)
486-555-0150	Weapons (Poor)

Grand Theft Auto 4

PASSWORDS

Cell Phone Passwords

At any time during the game, pull out Niko's phone and dial these numbers for the desired effect.

Please note that cheats will affect missions and achievements.

Password	Effect
468-555-0100	Change weather
486-555-0150	Get a different selection of weapons
486-555-0100	Get a selection of weapons
267-555-0150	Raise wanted level
267-555-0100	Remove wanted level
362-555-0100	Restore armour
482-555-0100	Restore health, armor, and ammo
948-555-0100	Song information
227-555-0142	Spawn a Cognoscenti
227-555-0175	Spawn a Comet
938-555-0100	Spawn a Jetmax
625-555-0150	Spawn a Sanchez
227-555-0168	Spawn a SuperGT
227-555-0147	Spawn a Turismo
359-555-0100	Spawn an Annihiliator

Password	Effect
227-555-0100	Spawn an FIB Buffalo
625-555-0100	Spawn an NRG-900

Map Locations

Enter the following password into the in-game computers.

Password	Effect
www.whattheydonotwantyoutoknow.com	Weapon, health, armor, vehicle, pigeon, ramp/stunt, and entertainment locations

Grand Theft Auto Episodes From Liberty City

CODES

Cheat Codes

Dial these codes into your cell phone during game play.

Code	Effect
625-555-0200	Akuma (Bike)
272-555-8265	APC(Tank)
359-555-2899	Buzzard(Helicopter)
468-555-0100	Change Weather
938-555-0150	Floater(Boat)
362-555-0100	Health & Armour
482-555-0100	Health, Armor and Advanced Weapons
359-555-7272	Parachute
267-555-0150	Raise Wanted Level
267-555-0100	Remove Wanted Level
486-555-2526	Sniper rifle bullets explode
359-555-0100	Spawn Annihilator
227-555-9666	Spawn Bullet GT
227-555-0142	Spawn Cognoscenti
227-555-0175	Spawn Comet

Code	Effect
938-555-0100	Spawn Jetmax
625-555-0100	Spawn NRG-900
625-555-0150	Spawn Sanchez
227-555-0168	Spawn Super GT
227-555-0147	Spawn Turismo
227-555-0100	Spawns a FIB Buffalo
276-555-2666	Super Punch (exploding punches)
625-555-3273	Vader(Bike)
486-555-0100	Weapons (New & advanced)
486-555-0150	Weapons (Poor)

CODES

Spawn Vehicles

Bring out your cell phone and input the following phone numbers.

Code	Effect
227-555-0142	Spawn a Cognoscenti
227-555-0175	Spawn a Comet
227-555-0100	Spawn a FIB Buffalo
938-555-0100	Spawn a Jetmax
625-555-0150	Spawn a Sanchez
227-555-0147	Spawn a Turismo

Code	Effect
625-555-0100	Spawn an NRG-900
359-555-0100	Spawn Annihilator
826-555-0150	Spawn Burrito
245-555-0125	Spawn Double T
245-555-0199	Spawn Hakuchou
245-555-0150	Spawn Hexer
245-555-0100	Spawn Innovation
826-555-0100	Spawn Slamvan

Grand Theft Auto 5

CODES

Cheat Codes

Warning: These cheats disable earning Trophies while activated.

Code	Effect
Left, Right, L1, L2, R1, R2, R2, Left, Left, Right, L1	Give Item: Parachute
Triangle, R2, Left, L1, X, Right, Triangle, Down, Square, L1, L1, L1	Give Weapons (Tier 1)
O, L1, Triangle, R2, X, Square, O, Right, Square, L1, L1, L1	Max Health and Armor
Triangle, Right, Right, Left, Right, Square, O, Left	Player Cheat: Drunk
Right, Left, X, Triangle, R1, O, O, O, L2	Player Cheat: Explosive Melee Attacks
Right, Square, X, Left, R1, R2, Left, Right, Right, L1, L1, L1	Player Cheat: Explosive Rounds
Triangle, Left, Right, Right, L2, L1, Square	Player Cheat: Fast Run
Left, Left, L1, Right, Right, R2, Left, L2, Right	Player Cheat: Fast Swim
L1, R1, Square, R1, Left, R2, R1, Left, Square, Right, L1, L1	Player Cheat: Flame Rounds
Right, X, Right, Left, Right, R1, Right, Left, X, Triangle	Player Cheat: Invincibility
X, X, Square, R1, L1, X, Right, Left, X	Player Cheat: Recharge Special Ability
L1, L2, R1, R2, Left, Right, Left, Right, L1, L2, R1, R2, Left, Right, Left, Right	Player Cheat: Skyfall
Square, L2, R1, Triangle, Left, Square, L2, Right, X	Player cheat: slo mo aiming
L2, L2, Square, O, O, L2, Square, Square, Left, Right, X	Player Cheat: Super Jump
R1, R1, O, R2, Right, Left, Right, Left, Right, Left	Player Cheat: Wanted Level

Code	Effect
	- Lower
R1, R1, O, R2, Left, Right, Left, Right, Left, Right	Player Cheat: Wanted Level - Raise
Left, Left, Right, Right, Left, Right, Square, O, Triangle, R1, R2	Spawn Vehicle: BMX
O, O, L1, O, O, O, L1, L2, R1, Triangle, O, Triangle	Spawn Vehicle: Buzzard
O, L1, Left, R1, L2, X, R1, L1, O, X	Spawn Vehicle: Caddy
R1, O, R2, Right, L1, L2, X, X, Square, R1	Spawn Vehicle: Comet
Right, Left, R1, R1, R1, Left, Triangle, Triangle, X, O, L1, L1	Spawn Vehicle: Duster
R2, Right, L2, Left, Left, R1, L1, O, Right	Spawn Vehicle: Limo
R1, Right, Left, Right, R2, Left, Right, Square, Right, L2, L1, L1	Spawn Vehicle: PCJ-600
R2, L1, O, Right, L1, R1, Right, Left, O, R2	Spawn Vehicle: Rapid GT
O, X, L1, O, O, L1, O, R1, R2, L2, L1, L1	Spawn Vehicle: Sanchez
O, Right, L1, L2, Left, R1, L1, L1, Left, Left, X, Triangle	Spawn Vehicle: Stunt Plane
O, R1, O, R1, Left, Left, R1, L1, O, Right	Spawn Vehicle: Trashmaster
R2, X, L1, L1, L2, L2, L2, Square	World Cheat: Change Weather
Left, Left, L1, R1, L1, Right, Left, L1, Left	World Cheat: Moon Gravity*
Triangle, R1, R1, Left, R1, L1, R2, L1	World Cheat: Slippery Streets
Triangle, Left, Right, Right, Square, R2, R1	World Cheat: Slow Motion

PS4

Grand Theft Auto 5

CODES

Cell Phone Cheats

Open the dial-pad in the cell phone to enter cheats.

Code	Effect
1-999-625-348-7246	Change Weather
1-999-547-861	Drunk Mode
1-999-444-439	Explosive Bullets
1-999-462-842-637	Explosive Melee Attack
1-999-228-8463	Fast Run
1-999-462-363-4279	Flaming Bullets
1-999-759-3483	Give Parachute
1-999-724-654-5537	Invincibility
1-999-5299-3787	Lower Wanted Level
1-999-887-853	Max Health And Armor
1-999-356-2837	Moon Gravity
1-999-384-48483	Raise Wanted Level
1-999-769-3787	Recharge Special Ability
1-999-759-3255	Skydive
1-999-766-9329	Slippery Cars (Drifting)

Code	Effect
1-999-332-3393	Slow Aiming (Enter 4 times to increase effect, 5th time disables cheat)
1-999-756-966	Slow Motion (Enter 3 times to increase effect, 4th time disables cheat)
1-999-226-348	Spawn BMX
1-999-289-9633	Spawn Buzzard
1-999-26638	Spawn Comet
1-999-398-4628	Spawn Dodo Airplane
1-999-3328-4227	Spawn Dukes O'Death
1-999-282-2537	Spawn Kraken Sub
1-999-846-39663	Spawn Limo
1-999-762-538	Spawn PCJ-600
1-999-727-4348	Spawn Rapid GT
1-999-633-7623	Spawn Sanchez
1-999-227-678-676	Spawn Stunt Plane
1-999-872-7433	Spawn Trashmaster

GTA V button press cheats.

Enter the button combination corresponding to the desired cheat during gameplay or in the pause menu to activate cheat. If you entered a cheat correctly, a small confirmation will appear above the map.

Code	Effect
R2, X, L1, L1, L2, L2, L2, Square	Change Weather (Enter multiple times to cycle weather)
Triangle, Right, Right, Left, Right, Square, Circle, Left	Drunk Mode
Right, Square, X, Left, R1, R2, Left, Right, Right, L1, L1, L1	Explosive Ammo Rounds
Right, Left, X, Triangle, R1, Circle, Circle, Circle, L2	Explosive Melee Attacks
Triangle, Left, Right, Right, L2, L1, Square	Fast Run
Left, Left, L1, Right, Right, R2, Left, L2, Right	Fast Swim
L1, R1, Square, R1, Left, R2, R1, Left, Square, Right, L1, L1	Flaming Bullets
Right, X, Right, Left, Right, R1, Right, Left, X, Triangle	Invincibility (For 5 minutes)
Triangle, R1, R1, Left, R1, L1, R2, L1	Less Vehicle Traction
R1, R1, Circle, R2, Right, Left, Right, Left, Right, Left	Lower Wanted Level
Circle, L1, Triangle, R2, X, Square, Circle, Right, Square, L1, L1, L1	Max Health & Armor
Left, Left, L1, R1, L1, Right, Left, L1, Left	Moon Gravity
Left, Right, L1, L2, R1, R2, R2, Left, Left, Right, L1	Parachute
R1, R1, Circle, R2, Left, Right, Left, Right, Left, Right	Raise Wanted Level
X, X, Square, R1, L1, X, Right, Left, X	Recharge Ability
L1, L2, R1, R2, Left, Right, Left, Right, L1, L2, R1, R2, Left, Right, Left, Right	Skyfall
Triangle, Left, Right, Right, Square, R2, R1	Slow Motion (Can enter up to 3 times for

Code	Effect
	compounded effect, 4th time disables effect)
Square, L2, R1, Triangle, Left, Square, L2, Right, X	Slow Motion Aim (Can enter up to 4 times to compounded effect, 5th time disables effect)
Left, Left, Right, Right, Left, Right, Square, Circle, Triangle, R1, R2	Spawn BMX
Circle, Circle, L1, Circle, Circle, Circle, L1, L2, R1, Triangle, Circle, Triangle	Spawn Buzzard (Attack Helicopter)
Circle, L1, Left, R1, L2, X, R1, L1, Circle, X	Spawn Caddy
R1, Circle, R2, Right, L1, L2, X, X, Square, R1	Spawn Comet
Right, Left, R1, R1, R1, Left, Triangle, Triangle, X, Circle, L1, L1	Spawn Duster
R2, Right, L2, Left, Left, R1, L1, Circle, Right	Spawn Limo
Circle, Circle, Square, Square, Triangle, Triangle L1, L2, R1, R2	Spawn Money Bags
R1, Right, Left, Right, R2, Left, Right, Square Right, L2, L1, L1	Spawn PCJ-600
R2, L1, Circle, Right, L1, R1, Right, Left, Circle, R2	Spawn Rapid GT
Circle, X, L1, Circle, Circle, L1, Circle, R1, R2, L2, L1, L1	Spawn Sanchez
Circle, Right, L1, L2, Left, R1, L1, L1, Left, Left, X, Triangle	Spawn Stunt Plane
Circle, R1, Circle, R1, Left, Left, R1, L1, Circle, Right	Spawn Trashmaster
Left, Left, Triangle, Triangle, Right, Right, Left, Right, Square, R1, R2	Super Jump (Hold square for greater jump)
Triangle, R2, Left, L1, X, Right, Triangle, Down, Square, L1, L1, L1	Weapons

Xbox

Grand Theft Auto 3

Enter all these cheats during gameplay. It is advised that you do not save with cheats enabled.

All Weapons:

Black, Black, L, Black, Left, Down, Right, Up, Left, Down, Right, Up

Full Health:

Black, Black, L, R, Left, Down, Right, Up, Left, Down, Right, Up

Full Armor:

Black, Black, L, White, Left, Down, Right, Up, Left, Down, Right, Up

Raise Wanted Level:

Black, Black, L, Black, Left, Right, Left, Right, Left, Right.

Lower Wanted Level:

Black, Black, L, Black, Up, Down, Up, Down, Up, Down.

More Money ($250,000):

Black, Black, L, L, Left, Down, Right, Up, Left, Down, Right, Up

Spawn a Tank:

B, B, B, B, B, B, R, White, L, Y, B, Y.

Speed Up Time:

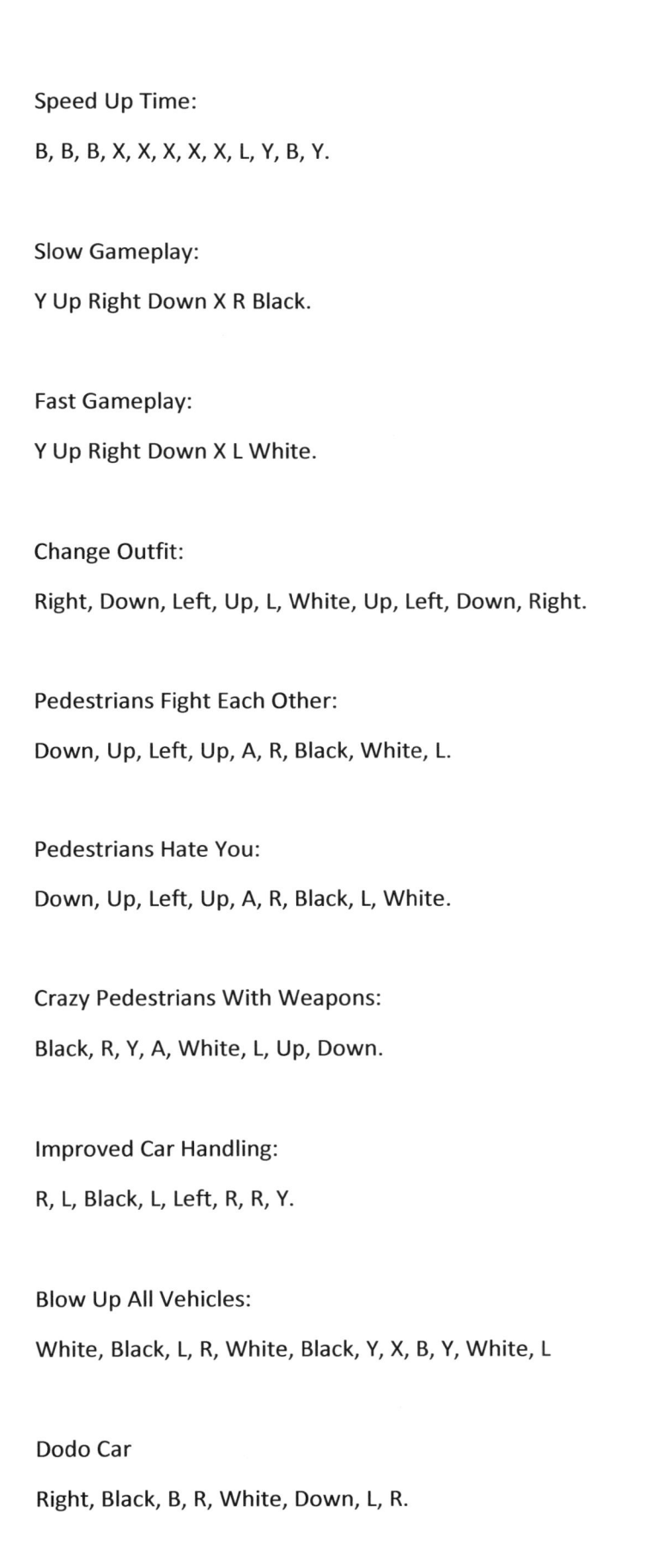

B, B, B, X, X, X, X, X, L, Y, B, Y.

Slow Gameplay:

Y Up Right Down X R Black.

Fast Gameplay:

Y Up Right Down X L White.

Change Outfit:

Right, Down, Left, Up, L, White, Up, Left, Down, Right.

Pedestrians Fight Each Other:

Down, Up, Left, Up, A, R, Black, White, L.

Pedestrians Hate You:

Down, Up, Left, Up, A, R, Black, L, White.

Crazy Pedestrians With Weapons:

Black, R, Y, A, White, L, Up, Down.

Improved Car Handling:

R, L, Black, L, Left, R, R, Y.

Blow Up All Vehicles:

White, Black, L, R, White, Black, Y, X, B, Y, White, L

Dodo Car

Right, Black, B, R, White, Down, L, R.

Increased Gore Mode:

X, L, B, Down, L, R, Y, Right, L, A.

No confirmation message will appear

Clear Weather:

L, White, R, Black, Black, R, White, Y.

Foggy Weather:

L, White, R, Black, Black, R, White, A.

Cloudy Weather:

L, White, R, Black, Black, R, White, X.

Rainy Weather:

L, White, R, Black, Black, R, White, B.

Grand Theft Auto Vice City

Enter all cheats while in-game. It is recommended you do not save with cheats on.

Player Cheats

All Weapons #1
R, Black, L, Black, Left, Down, Right, Up, Left, Down, Right, Up

All Weapons #2
R, Black, L, Black, Left, Down, Right, Up, Left, Down, Down, Left

All Weapons #3
R, Black, L, Black, Left, Down, Right, Up, Left, Down, Down, Down

Full Armor
R, Black, L, A, Left, Down, Right, Up, Left, Down, Right, Up

Full Health
R, Black, L, B, Left, Down, Right, Up, Left, Down, Right, Up

Commit Suicide
Right, White, Down, R, Left, Left, R, L, White, L

Raise Wanted Level
R, R, B, Black, Left, Right, Left, Right, Left, Right

Lower Wanted Level
R, R, B, Black, Up, Down, Up, Down, Up, Down

Ladies Man (certain women follow you)
B, A, L, L, Black, A, A, B, Y

Character Skin Cheats

Change Clothes
Right, Right, Left, Up, L, White, Left, Up, Down, Right

Play As Ricardo Diaz
L, White, R, Black, Down, L, Black, White

Play As Lance Vance

B, White, Left, A, R, L, A, L

Play As Candy Suxxx
B, Black, Down, R, Left, Right, R, L, A, White

Play As Ken Rosenberg
Right, L, Up, White, L, Right, R, L, A, R

Play As Hilary King
R, B, Black, L, Right, R, L, A, Black

Play As Love Fist Guy #1
Down, L, Down, White, Left, A, R, L, A, A

Play As Love Fist Guy #2
R, White, Black, L, Right, Black, Left, A, X, L

Play As Phil Cassady
Right, R, Up, Black, L, Right, R, L, Right, B

Play As Sonny Forelli
B, L, B, White, Left, A, R, L, A, A

Play As Mercedes
Black, L, Up, L, Right, R, Right, Up, B, Y

Vehicle Spawning Cheats

Spawn A Rhino
B, B, L, B, B, B, L, White, R, Y, B, Y

Spawn A Bloodring Banger 1
Down, R, B, White, White, A, R, L, Left, Left

Spawn A Bloodring Banger 2
Up, Right, Right, L, Right, Up, X, White

Spawn A Hotring Racer #1
R, B, Black, Right, L, White, A, A, X, R

Spawn A Hotring Racer #2
Black, L, B, Right, L, R, Right, Up, B, Black

Spawn A Romero's Hearse

Down, Black, Down, R, White, Left, R, L, Left, Right

Spawn A Love Fist
Black, Up, White, Left, Left, R, L, B, Right

Spawn A Trashmaster
B, R, B, R, Left, Left, R, L, B, Right

Spawn A Sabre Turbo
Right, White, Down, White, White, A, R, L, B, Left

Spawn A Caddie
B, L, Up, R, White, A, R, L, B, A

Other Vehicle Cheats

Blow Up Cars
Black, White, R, L, White, Black, X, Y, B, Y, White, L

Aggressive Drivers
Black, B, R, White, Left, R, L, Black, White

Pink Cars
B, L, Down, White, Left, A, R, L, Right, A

Pink Cars
B, L, Down, White, Left, A, R, L, Right, B

Black Cars
B, White, Up, R, Left, A, R, L, Left, B

Dodo Cheat (Press Analog Stick back to Fly)
Right, Black, B, R, White, Down, L, R

Perfect Handling
Y, R, R, Left, R, L, Black, L

Higher Top Speed For Your vehicle
Right, R, Up, White, White, Left, R, L, R, R

Cars Can Drive on Water
Right, Black, B, R, White, X, R, Black

Change Vehicle Wheel Size (Repeat to change more)
R, A, Y, Right, Black, X, Up, Down, X

Weather Cheats

Sunny Weather
Black, A, L, L, White, White, White, Down

Cloudy Weather
Black, A, L, L, White, White, White, Y

Very Cloudy Weather
Black, A, L, L, White, White, White, X

Stormy Weather
Black, A, L, L, White, White, White, B

Foggy Weather
Black, A, L, L, White, White, White, A

Miscellaneous Cheats

Speed Up Time
B, B, L, X, L, X, X, X, L, Y, B, Y

Slow Down Time
Y, Up, Right, Down, X, Black, R

Peds Riot - (Warning code cannot be undone)
Down, Left, Up, Left, A, Black, R, White, L

Peds Hate You - (Warning code cannot be undone)
Down, Up, Up, Up, A, Black, R, White, White

Peds have Weapons - (Warning code cannot be undone)
Black, R, A, Y, A, Y, Up, Down

Police return From Dead
B, L, Down, White, Left, A, R, L, Right, A

Show Media Level Meter (Shows pursuit time and news coverage level)
Black, B, Up, L, Right, R, Right, Up, X, Y

Bikini Girls With Guns
Right, L, B, White, Left, A, R, L, L, A

Suicide
White, Down, R, Left, Left, R, L, White, L

Grand Theft Auto SanAndreas

Cheat codes

Enter these codes in game. (Use the D-Pad, not the analog stick). You will see the message, Cheat Activated, if entered properly.

Code	Effect
R Trigger, Black, L Trigger , A, Left , Down, Right, Up, Left, Down, Right, Up	$250,000 + Full Health & Armor
B, Right, B, Right, Left, X, A Down	Add Six Stars to Wanted Level
RIGHT, Black, UP, UP, Black, B, X, Black, L Trigger, RIGHT, DOWN, L Trigger	Aggressive Drivers
Black, B, R Trigger, White, Left R Trigger, L Trigger, Black, White	Aggressive Traffic
LEFT, Y, R Trigger, L Trigger, UP, X, Y, DOWN, B, White, L Trigger, L Trigger	All Cars Have Nitrous
L Trigger, White, White, Up, Down, Down, Up, R Trigger, Black, Black	All Cars have Tank Properties.
White, RIGHT, L Trigger, UP, A, L Trigger, White, Black, R Trigger, L Trigger, L Trigger, L Trigger	All Traffic are Junk Cars
L Trigger, L Trigger, R Trigger, R Trigger White, L Trigger, Black, Down, Left, Up	All Vehicles are Farm Vehicles
Y, L Trigger, Y, Black, X, L Trigger, L Trigger	All Vehicles are Invisible (Not Motorcycles)
X, L Trigger, R Trigger, RIGHT, A, UP, L Trigger, LEFT, LEFT	Always Midnight
A, A, X, R Trigger, L Trigger, A, Down, Left, A	Andrenaline Mode
X, Right, X, X, White, A, Y, A, Y	Attracts Prostitutes (Pimp Mode)
X, X, Black, Left, Up, X, Black, A, A, A	Better Suspension

Code	Effect
Up, Up, Down, Down, X, B, L Trigger, R Trigger, Y, Down	Bikini Beach Babe Mode
B, White, Up, R Trigger, Left, A, R Trigger, L Trigger, Left, B	Black Traffic
X, Down, White, Up, L Trigger, B, Up, A, Left	Cars Can Fly
Right, Black, B, R Trigger, White, X, R Trigger, Black	Cars Drive on Water (Boat Properties)
X, Black, Down, Down, Left, Down, Left, Left, White, A	Cars Fly Away When Hit
White, RIGHT, L Trigger, Y, RIGHT, RIGHT, R Trigger, L Trigger, RIGHT, L Trigger, L Trigger, L Trigger	Chaos mode
White, DOWN, DOWN, LEFT, X, LEFT, Black, X, A, R Trigger, L Trigger, L Trigger	Cloudy
Black, White, R Trigger, L Trigger, White, Black, X, Y, B, Y, White, L Trigger	Destroy All Cars
Right, R Trigger, Up, White, White, Left, R Trigger, L Trigger, R Trigger, R Trigger	Faster Cars
B, B, L Trigger, X, L Trigger, X, X, X, L Trigger, Y, B, Y	Faster Clock
Y, Up, Right, Down, White, L Trigger, X	Faster Gameplay
Black, B, Up, L Trigger, Right, R Trigger, Right, Up, X, Y	Flying Boats
Black, A, L Trigger, L Trigger, White, White, White, A	Foggy
up, up, X, White, right, A, R Trigger, down, Black, B	Full Weapon Aiming While Driving
Left, Right, L Trigger, White, R Trigger, Black, Up, Down, Left, Right	Have Jetpack
DOWN, X, A, LEFT, R Trigger, Black, LEFT, DOWN, DOWN, L Trigger, L Trigger, L Trigger	Hitman Rank (All Weapons)
up, L Trigger, R Trigger, up, right, up, A, White, A, L Trigger	Increase Car Speed
L Trigger, R Trigger, X, R Trigger, LEFT, Black, R Trigger, LEFT, X,	Infinite Ammo

Code	Effect
DOWN, L Trigger, L Trigger	
Down, A, Right, Left, Right, R Trigger, Right, Down, Up, Y	Infinite health (Explosions, drowning, and falling will still hurt.)
Right, White, Down, R Trigger, Left, Left, R Trigger, L Trigger, White, L Trigger	KILL YOURSELF (INSANT DEATH!!!)
Y, Y, L Trigger, X, X, B, X, Down, B	Killer Clown Mode
B, RIGHT, B, RIGHT, LEFT, X, Y, UP	Lock Wanted Level
R Trigger, R Trigger, B, Black, Up, Down, Up, Down, Up, Down	Lower Wanted Level
Y, Up, Up, Left, Right, X, B, Down	Max Fat
Y, Up, Up, Left, Right, X, B, Left	Max Muscle
L Trigger, R Trigger, Y, DOWN, Black, A, L Trigger, UP, White, White, L Trigger, L Trigger	Max Respect
B, Y, Y, UP, B, R Trigger, White, UP, Y, L Trigger, L Trigger, L Trigger	Max Sex Appeal
Up, A, Y, A, Y, A, X, Black, Right	Max Stamina
X, White, A, R Trigger, White, White, LEFT, R Trigger, RIGHT, L Trigger, L Trigger, L Trigger	Max Vehicle Stats
Black, A, L Trigger, L Trigger, White, White, White, X	Morning
X, White, R Trigger, Y, UP, X, White, UP, A	Never Hungry
Black, A, L Trigger, L Trigger, White, White, White, Y	Night
Y, Up, Up, Left, Right, X, B, Right	No Muscle and No Fat
A, Down, Up, Black, Down, Y, L Trigger, Y, Left	No Pedestrians / Low Traffic
White, Up, R Trigger, R Trigger, Left, R Trigger, R Trigger, Black, Right, Down	No Pedestrians or Cops (Gan Riots)

Code	Effect
Black, A, L Trigger, L Trigger, White, White, White, Down	Noon
Left, Left, White, R Trigger, Right, X, X, L Trigger, White, A	Orange Sky
Black, A, L Trigger, L Trigger, White, White, White, X	Overcast
Left, Right, L Trigger, White, R Trigger, Black, Black, Up, Down, Right, L Trigger	Parachute
Down, Up, Up, Up, A, Black, R Trigger, White, White	Pedestrian Attack (Cant be Turned Off!!)
Down, Left, Up, Left, A, Black, R Trigger, White, L Trigger	Pedestrian Riot Mode (Cant be turned off!!)
L Trigger, B, Y, L Trigger, L Trigger, X, White, Up, Down, Left	Pedestrians Are Elvis
A, L Trigger, UP, X, DOWN, A, White, Y, DOWN, R Trigger, L Trigger, L Trigger	Pedestrians Attack with Guns
Black, R Trigger, A, Y, A, Y, Up, Down	Pedestrians have weapons
Y, R Trigger, R Trigger, Left, R Trigger, L Trigger, Black, L Trigger	Perfect Handling in Vehicles
B, L Trigger, Down, White, Left, A, R Trigger, L Trigger, Right, B	Pink Traffic
Right, White, White, Down, White, Up, Up, White, Black	Prostitutes pay you (Pimp Mode 2)
R Trigger, R Trigger, B, Black, Right, Left, Right, Left, Right, Left	Raise Wanted Level
DOWN, X, UP, Black, Black, UP, RIGHT, RIGHT, UP	Recruit Anyone (9mm)
Black, Black, Black, A, White, L Trigger, Black, L Trigger, DOWN, A	Recruit Anyone (Rockets)
Up, Down, L Trigger, L Trigger, White, White, L Trigger, White, R Trigger, Black	Sand Storm
Y, Up, Up, Left, Right, X, B, Right	Skinny
Y, Up, Right, Down, X, Black, R Trigger	Slow down Game Play

Code	Effect
Down, R Trigger, B, White, White, A, R Trigger, L Trigger, Left, Left	Spawn Bloodring Banger
B, L Trigger, Up, R Trigger, White, A, R Trigger, L Trigger, B, A	Spawn Caddy
Black, L Trigger, L Trigger, RIGHT, RIGHT, UP, UP, A, L Trigger, LEFT	Spawn Dozer
R Trigger, B, Black, Right, L Trigger, White, A, A, X, R Trigger	Spawn Hotring Racer #1
Black, L Trigger, B, Right, L Trigger, R Trigger, Right, Up, B, Black	Spawn Hotring Racer #2
B, A, L Trigger, B, B, L Trigger, B, R Trigger, Black, White, L Trigger, L Trigger	Spawn Hunter
Y, Y, X, B, A, L Trigger, L Trigger, Down, Up	Spawn Hydra
Right, Up, R Trigger, R Trigger, R Trigger, Down, Y, Y, A, B, L Trigger, L Trigger	Spawn Monster
Left, Left, Down, Down, Up, Up, X, B, Y, R Trigger, Black	Spawn Quadbike
Up, Right, Right, L Trigger, Right, Up, X, White	Spawn Rancher
B, B, L Trigger, B, B, B, L Trigger, White, R Trigger, Y, B, Y	Spawn Rhino
Black, Up, White, Left, Left, R Trigger, L Trigger, B, Right	Spawn Stretch
B, Up, L Trigger, White, Down, R Trigger, L Trigger, L Trigger, Left, Left, A, Y	Spawn Stunt Plane
R Trigger, UP, LEFT, RIGHT, Black, UP, RIGHT, X, RIGHT, White, L Trigger, L Trigger	Spawn Tanker
Y, Y, X, B, A, L Trigger, White, Down, Down	Spawn Vortex
Black, A, L Trigger, L Trigger, White, White, White, B	Stormy
Y, X, B, B, X, B, B, L Trigger, White, White, R Trigger, Black	Super Bike Jumps
Up, Up, Y, Y, Up, Up, Left, Right, X, Black, Black	Super Jumps
Down, Left, L Trigger, Down, Down, Black, Down, White, Down	Super Lung Capacity (Infinite Air)

Code	Effect
Up, Left, A, Y, R Trigger, B, B, B, White	Super Punches
Y, Left, X, White, Up, Black, Down, L Trigger, A, L Trigger, L Trigger, L Trigger	Traffic becomes Farm Vehicles
Right, R Trigger, Up, White, White, Left, R Trigger, L Trigger, R Trigger, R Trigger	Traffic Lights Stay Green
Down, Black, Down, R Trigger, White, Left, R Trigger, L Trigger, Left, Right	Unlock Romero
B, R Trigger, B, R Trigger, Left, Left, R Trigger, L Trigger, B, Right	Unlock Trashmaster
R Trigger, Black, L Trigger, Black, Left, Down, Right, Up, Left, Down, Right, Up	Weapon Set 1
R Trigger, Black, L Trigger, Black, Left, Down, Right, Up, Left, Down, Down, Left	Weapon Set 2
R Trigger, Black, L Trigger, Black, Left, Down, Right, Up, Left , Down, Down, Down	Weapon Set 3
A, A, Down, Black, White, B. R Trigger, B, X	Yakuza Mode (Peds & cars are Asian Gang)

Xbox One

Grand Theft Auto 5

Cell Phone Cheat Codes

In Single Player only, pull up your phone, from there select your contacts, then press X. bringing up the dial pad and enter the code you want.

Code	Effect
1-999-4684-2637 (HOTHANDS)	Explosive Melle attacks
1-999-444-439 (HIGHEX)	Explosive rounds for all weapons
1-999-462-363-4279 (INCENDIARY)	Flaming Bullets
1-999-759-3483 (SKY-DIVE)	Give Parachute
1-999-356-2837 (FLOATER)	Moon Gravity
1-999-769-3787 (POWER-UP)	Recharge Ability
1-999-759-3255 (SKY-FALL)	Skyfall
1-999-7569-66 (SLOW-MO)	Slow Down Gameplay
1-999-756-966 (SLOW-MO)	Slow Motion (enter 3 times for more effect)
1-999-332-3393 (DEAD-EYE)	Slow Motion Aiming (enter 3 times for more effect)
1-999-289-9633 (BUZZ-OFF)	Spawn Buzzard Attack Chopper
1-999-266-38 (COMET)	Spawn Comet
1-999-846-39663 (VINEWOOD)	Spawn Limo
1-999-762-538 (ROCKET)	Spawn PCJ-600 Motorcycle

Code	Effect
1-999-727-4348 (RAPID-GT)	Spawn Rapid GT
1-999-633-7623 (OFF-ROAD)	Spawn Sanchez Dirt Bike
1-999-872-433 (TRASHED)	Spawn Trashmaster

Xbox 360

Grand Theft Auto SanAndreas

Codes

Enter the codes while playing the game. Codes will eliminate achievements.

Code	Effect
RT, RB, LT, A, Left, Down, Right, Up, Left, Down, Right, Up	$250,000 + Full Health, & Full Armor
B, Right, B, Right, Left, X, A Down	Add Stars to Wanted Level
A, A, X, RT, LT, A, Down, Left, A	Adrenaline Effects
Right, RB, Up, Up, RB, B, X, RB, LT, Right, Down, LT	Aggressive Drivers
RB, B, RT, LB, Left RT, LT, RB, LB	Aggressive Traffic
Left, Y, RT, LT, Up, X, Y, Down, B, LB, LT, LT	All Cars Have Nitrous
LT, LB, LB, Up, Down, Down, Up, RT, RB, RB	All Cars have Tank Properties
LB, Right, LT, Up, A, LT, LB, RB, RT, LT, LT, LT	All Traffic are Junk Cars
Right, RT, Up, LB, LB, Left, RT, LT, RT, RT	All Traffic Lights Remain Green
Y, LT, Y, RB, X, LT, LT	All Vehicles are Invisible (Not Motorcycles)
X, LT, RT, Right, A, Up, LT, Left, Left	Always 00:00 or 12:00
Left, Left, LB, RT, Right, X, X, LT, LB, A	Always 21:00
X, LT, RT, Right, A, Up, LT, Left, Left	Always Midnight
A, A, X, RT, LT, A, Down, Left, A	Andrenaline Mode

Code	Effect
X, Right, X, X, LB, A, Y, A, Y	Attracts Prostitutes - (Pimp Mode)
Up, Up, Down, Down, X, B, LT, RT, Y, Down	Beach Party Theme
LB, Right, LT, Up, A, LT, LB, RB, RT, LT, LT, LT	Beater Traffic
X, X, RB, Left, Up, X, RB, A, A, A	Better Suspension
Up, Up, Down, Down, X, B, L TRIGGER, RT, Y, Down	Bikini Beach Babe Mode
B, LB, Up, RT, Left, A, RT, LT, Left, B	Black Traffic
Down, Up, Up, Up, A, RB, RT, LB, LB	Bounty on CJ
Y, Y, LT, X, X, B, X, Down, B	Carnival Theme
X, Down, LB, Up, LT, B, Up, A, Left	Cars Can Fly
Right, RB, B, RT, LB, X, RT, RB	Cars Drive on Water (Boat Properties)
X, RB, Down, Down, Left, Down, Left, Left, LB, A	Cars Fly Away When Hit
LB, Right, LT, Y, Right, Right, RT, LT, Right, LT, LT, LT	City in Chaos
Up, Up, Y, Y, Up, Up, Left, Right, X, RB, RB	CJ Jumps Higher
RT, RT, B, RB, Up, Down, Up, Down, Up, Down	Clear Wanted Level
Up, A, Y, A, Y, A, X, RB, Right	Click Left Thumb Stick to make cars jump
Down, Down, Left, X, Left, RB, X, A, RT, LT, LT	Cloudy LB
LB, Down, Down, Left, X, Left, RB, X, A, RT, LT, LT	Cloudy Weather
Right, LB, Down, RT, Left, Left, RT, LT, LB, LT	Commit Suicide
LT, LB, LB, Up, Down, Down, Up, RT, RB, RB	Death Car
RB, LB, RT, LT, LB, RB, X, Y, B, Y, LB, LT	Destroy All Cars

Code	Effect
Y, Up, Right, Down, LB, LT, X	Fast Motion
Right, RT, Up, LB, LB, Left, RT, LT, RT, RT	Faster Cars
B, B, LT, X, LT, X, X, X, LT, Y, B, Y	Faster Clock
RB, B, Up, LT, Right, RT, Right, Up, X, Y	Flying Boats
RB, A, LT, LT, LB, LB, LB, A	Foggy Weather
B, Right, B, Right, Left, X, Down	Full Wanted Level
LB, Up, RT, RT, Left, RT, RT, RB, Right, Down	Gangs Only
Down, X, A, Left, RT, RB, Left, Down, Down, LT, LT, LT	Hitman Level for all Weapons
LT, RT, X, RT, Left, RB, RT, Left, X, Down, LT, LT	Infinite Ammo
X, Right, X, X, LB, A, Y, A, Y	Kinky Theme
B, Right, B, right, Left, X, Y, Up	Lock Wanted Level
Y, X, B, B, X, B, B, LT, LB, LB, RT, RB	Massive BMX Bunny Hops
Y, Up, Up, Left, Right, X, B, Left	Max Muscle
LT, RT, Y, Down, RB, A, LT, Up, LB, LB, LT, LT	Max Respect
Y, Up, Up, Left, Right, X, B, Down	Maximum Fat
B, Y, Y, Up, B, RT, LB, Up, Y, LT, LT, LT	Maximum Sex Appeal
X, LB, A, RT, LB, LB, Left, RT, Right, LT, LT, LT	Maximum Vehicle Skills
Down, A, Right, Left, Right, RT, Right, Down, Up, Y	No Bullet Damage
Y, Up, Up, Left, Right, X, B, Right	No Fat or Muscle
RB, A, LT, LT, LB, LB, LB, Y	Overcast Weather
Down, Left, Up, A, RB, RT, LB, LT	Pedestrian Riot

Code	Effect
RB, RT, A, Y, A, Y, Up, Down	Pedestrians Have Weapons
Y, RT, RT, Left, RT, LT, RB, LT	Perfect Handling
Right, LB, LB, Down, LB, Up, Up, LB, RB	Pimping Missions Completed
B, LT, Down, LB, Left, A, RT, LT, Right, B	Pink Traffic
RT, RT, B, RB, Left, Right, Left, Right, Left, Right	Raise Wanted Level
B, LB, Up, RT, Left, A, RT, LT, Left, B	RB Traffic
LT, LT, RT, RT, LB, LT, RB, Down, Left, Up	Rural Theme
Y, Left, X, RB, Up, LB, Down, LT, A, LT, LT, LT	Rural Traffic
Up, Down, LT, LT, LB, LB, LT, LB, RT, RB	Sandstorm Weather
Y, Up, Right, Down, X, RB, RT	Slow Down Time
B, A, LT, B, B, LT, B, RT, RB, LB, LT, LT	Spawn Hunter
Y, Y, X, B, A, LT, LT, Down, Up	Spawn Hydra
Left, Right, LT, LB, RT, RB, Up, Down, Left, Right	Spawn Jetpack
B, B, LT, B, B, B, LT, LB, RT, Y, B, Y	Spawn Rhino
B, B, LT, B, B, B LT, LB, RT, Y, B, Y	Spawn Tank (Rhino)
Up, LT, RT, Up, Right, Up, A, LB, A, LT	Sports Car Traffic
RB, A, LT, LT, LB, LB, LB, B	Stormy Weather
RB, A, LT, LT, LB, LB, LB, Y	Sunny Weather
Up, Left, A, Y, RT, B, B, B, LB	Super Punches
Up, Left, Left, Down, B, X, LT, LT, LB, RT, RB	Taxi Missions Completed
RB, A, LT, LT, LB, LB, LB, X	Very Cloudy Weather

Code	Effect
RB, A, LT, LT, LB, LB, LB, Down	Very Sunny Weather
RT, RB, LT, RB, Left, Down, Right, Up, Left, Down, Right, Up	Weapon Set 1
RT, RB, LT, RB, Left, Down, Right, Up, Left, Down, Down, Left	Weapon Set 2
RT, RB, LT, RB, Left, Down, Right, Up, Left , Down, Down, Down	Weapon Set 3
A, A, Down, RB, LB, B, RT, B, X	Yakuza Theme

Grand Theft Auto: THE LOST AND DAMNED

Cheat codes for All Ranges, (NEW CODES)

Few codes based upon the new game, Some old codes work aswell.

Code	Effect
362-555-0100	Give Armor
482-555-0100	Gives Health, Armor And Ammo
267-555-0100	Lower Wanted Level
267-555-0150	Raise Wanted Level
486-555-0150	Weapon Package #1
486-555-0100	Weapon Package #2

Spawn Vehicles

Press "up" on the D-pad twice to take out your phone and enter these cheats:

Code	Effect
227-555-0142	Spawn a Cognoscenti
227-555-0175	Spawn a Comet
227-555-0100	Spawn a FIB Buffalo
938-555-0100	Spawn a Jetmax
625-555-0150	Spawn a Sanchez
227-555-0168	Spawn a Super GT
227-555-0147	Spawn a Turismo

Code	Effect
625-555-0100	Spawn an NRG-900
359-555-0100	Spawn Annihilator
826-555-0150	Spawn Burrito
245-555-0125	Spawn Double T
245-555-0199	Spawn Hakuchou
245-555-0150	Spawn Hexer
245-555-0100	Spawn Innovation
826-555-0100	Spawn Slamvan

Grand Theft Auto THE BALLAD OF GAY TONY

Cheat Codes

Dial these codes into your cell phone in game to gain the effect, go to the cheat menu in your cell phone to use previously entered cheats whenever.

Code	Effect
625-555-0200	Akuma (Bike)
272-555-8265	APC(Tank)
359-555-2899	Buzzard(Helicopter)
468-555-0100	Change Weather
938-555-0150	Floater(Boat)
362-555-0100	Health & Armour
482-555-0100	Health, Armor and Advanced Weapons
359-555-7272	Parachute
267-555-0150	Raise Wanted Level
267-555-0100	Remove Wanted Level
486-555-2526	Sniper rifle bullets explode
359-555-0100	Spawn Annihilator
227-555-9666	Spawn Bullet GT
227-555-0142	Spawn Cognoscenti
227-555-0175	Spawn Comet

Code	Effect
938-555-0100	Spawn Jetmax
625-555-0100	Spawn NRG-900
625-555-0150	Spawn Sanchez
227-555-0168	Spawn Super GT
227-555-0147	Spawn Turismo
227-555-0100	Spawns a FIB Buffalo
276-555-2666	Super Punch (exploding punches)
625-555-3273	Vader(Bike)
486-555-0100	Weapons (Advanced) (New Weapons)
486-555-0150	Weapons (Poor)

Grand Theft Auto 4

CODES

URLs

Go to an internet cafe and type in this URL

Code	Effect
www.love-meet.net	a dating website
www.vipluxuryringtones.com	free themes for Niko's phone & ringtones for $100 each
www.whattheydonotwantyoutoknow.com	Weapon, health, armor, vehicle, pigeon, ramp/stunt, and entertainment locations

PASSWORDS

Cell Phone Passwords

At any time during the game, pull out Niko's phone and dial these numbers for the desired effect.

Please note that cheats will affect missions and achievements.

Password	Effect
468-555-0100	Change weather
486-555-0150	Get a different selection of weapons
486-555-0100	Get a selection of weapons
267-555-0100	Lower wanted level
267-555-0150	Raise wanted level
362-555-0100	Restore armour
482-555-0100	Restore health, armor, and ammo
948-555-0100	Song information

Password	Effect
227-555-0142	Spawn a Cognoscenti
227-555-0175	Spawn a Comet
938-555-0100	Spawn a Jetmax
359-555-0100	Spawn a Police Chopper
625-555-0150	Spawn a Sanchez
227-555-0168	Spawn a SuperGT
227-555-0147	Spawn a Turismo
227-555-0100	Spawn an FIB Buffalo
625-555-0100	Spawn an NRG-900

Grand Theft Auto Episodes From Liberty City

Cheat Codes

Dial these codes into your cell phone in game to gain the effect, go to the cheat menu in your cell phone to use previously entered cheats whenever.

Code	Effect
625-555-0200	Akuma (Bike)
272-555-8265	APC(Tank)
359-555-2899	Buzzard(Helicopter)
468-555-0100	Change Weather
938-555-0150	Floater(Boat)
362-555-0100	Health & Armour
482-555-0100	Health, Armor and Advanced Weapons
359-555-7272	Parachute
267-555-0150	Raise Wanted Level
267-555-0100	Remove Wanted Level
486-555-2526	Sniper rifle bullets explode
359-555-0100	Spawn Annihilator
227-555-9666	Spawn Bullet GT
227-555-0142	Spawn Cognoscenti
227-555-0175	Spawn Comet

Code	Effect
938-555-0100	Spawn Jetmax
625-555-0100	Spawn NRG-900
625-555-0150	Spawn Sanchez
227-555-0168	Spawn Super GT
227-555-0147	Spawn Turismo
227-555-0100	Spawns a FIB Buffalo
276-555-2666	Super Punch (exploding punches)
625-555-3273	Vader(Bike)
486-555-0100	Weapons (Advanced) (New Weapons)
486-555-0150	Weapons (Poor)

Cheat codes for All Ranges, (NEW CODES)

Few codes based upon the new game, Some old codes work aswell.

Code	Effect
362-555-0100	Give Armor
482-555-0100	Gives Health, Armor And Ammo
267-555-0100	Lower Wanted Level
267-555-0150	Raise Wanted Level
486-555-0150	Weapon Package #1
486-555-0100	Weapon Package #2

Spawn Vehicles

Press "up" on the D-pad twice to take out your phone and enter these cheats:

Code	Effect
227-555-0142	Spawn a Cognoscenti
227-555-0175	Spawn a Comet
227-555-0100	Spawn a FIB Buffalo
938-555-0100	Spawn a Jetmax
625-555-0150	Spawn a Sanchez
227-555-0168	Spawn a Super GT
227-555-0147	Spawn a Turismo
625-555-0100	Spawn an NRG-900
359-555-0100	Spawn Annihilator
826-555-0150	Spawn Burrito
245-555-0125	Spawn Double T
245-555-0199	Spawn Hakuchou
245-555-0150	Spawn Hexer
245-555-0100	Spawn Innovation
826-555-0100	Spawn Slamvan

Grand Theft Auto 5

In Game Cheat Codes

Achievements are disabled when cheats are used. Enter during gameplay at any point of the map, or while in a Vehicle.

Code	Effect
Left, Right, LB, LT, RB, RT, RT, Left, Left, Right, LB	Give Item: Parachute
Right, A, Right, Left, Right, RB, Right, Left, A, Y	Player Cheat: 5 Minute Invincibility
Y, Right, Right, Left, Right, X, B, Left	Player Cheat: Drunk
Right, Left, A, Y, RB, B, B, B, LT	Player Cheat: Explosive Melee Attacks
Right, X, A, Left, RB, RT, Left, Right, Right, LB, LB, LB	Player Cheat: Explosive Rounds
Y, Left, Right, Right, LT, LB, X	Player Cheat: Fast Run
Left Left LB Right Right RT Left LT Right	Player Cheat: Fast Swim
LB, RB, X, RB, Left, RT, RB, Left, X, Right, LB, LB	Player Cheat: Flame Round
Y, RT, Left, LB, A, Right, Y, Down, X, LB, LB, LB	Player Cheat: Give Weapons/Ammo
B, LB, Y, RT, A, X, B, Right, X, LB, LB, LB	Player Cheat: Max Health & Armor
A, A, X, RB, LB, A, Right, Left, A	Player Cheat: Recharge Special Ability
LB, LT, RB, RT, LEFT, RIGHT, LEFT, RIGHT, LB, LT, RB, RT, LEFT, RIGHT, LEFT, RIGHT	Player Cheat: Skyfall (Spawn in the sky)
X LT RB Y Left X LT Right A	Player Cheat: Slo Mo Aiming

Code	Effect
Left, Left, Y, Y, Right, Right, Left, Right, X, RB, RT	Player Cheat: Super Jump
RB, RB, B, RT, Right, Left, Right, Left, Right, Left	Player Cheat: Wanted Level - Lower
RB, RB, B, RT, Left, Right, Left, Right, Left, Right	Player Cheat: Wanted Level - Raise
Left Left Right Right Left Right X B Y RB RT	Spawn Vehicle: BMX
B, B, LB, B, B, B, LB, LT, RB, Y, B, Y	Spawn Vehicle: Buzzard
B, LB, Left, RB, LT, A, RB, LB, B, A	Spawn Vehicle: Caddy
RB, B, RT, Right, LB, LT, A, A, X, RB	Spawn Vehicle: Comet
Right, Left, RB, RB, RB, Left, Y, Y, A, B, LB, LB	Spawn Vehicle: Duster
RT, Right, LT, Left, Left, RB, LB, B, Right	Spawn Vehicle: Limo
RB Right Left Right RT Left Right X Right LT LB LB	Spawn Vehicle: PCJ
RT, LB, B, Right, LB, RB, Right, Left, B, RT	Spawn Vehicle: Rapid GT
B, A, LB, B, B, LB, B, RB, RT, LT, LB, LB	Spawn Vehicle: Sanchez
B, Right, LB, LT, Left, RB, LB, LB, Left, Left, A, Y	Spawn Vehicle: Stunt Plane
B, RB, B, RB, Left, Left, RB, LB, B, Right	Spawn Vehicle: Trashmaster
RT, A, LB, LB, LT, LT, LT, X	World Cheat: Change Weather
Left Left LB RB LB Right Left LB Left	World Cheat: Moon Gravity
Y, RB, RB, Left, RB, LB, RT, LB	World Cheat: Slippery Streets
Y, Left, Right, Right, X, RT, RB	World Cheat: Slow Motion

Nintendo DS

Grand Theft Auto: Chinatown Wars

CODES

Enter these during gameplay without pausing:

Code	Effect
L, L, R, B, B, A, A, R	Armor
Up,Down,Left,Right,X,Y,L,R	cloud
L, R, X, Y, A, B, Up, Down	Explosive Pistol Round
Up, Down, Left, Right, B, X, L, R	Extra Sunny
Up, Down, Left, Right, Y, B, R, L	Fog
L,L,R,A,A,B,B,R	health
Up,Down,Left,Right,B,Y,R,L	Hurricane
Up,Down,Left,Right,A,X,R,L	lots of rain
Up,Down,Left,Right,Y,A,L,R	rain
Up,Down,Left,Right,A,B,L,R	sunny
R,X,X,Y,Y,R,L,L	wanted level down
L,L,R,Y,Y,X,X,R	wanted level up
R,Up,B,Down,Left,R,B,Right	weapons 1 (grenade, nightstick, pistol, minigun, assault, micro smg, stubby shotgun)
R,Up,A,Down,Left,R,A,Right	weapons 2 (molotov, teaser, dual pistols, flamethrower, carbine, smg, dual-barrel)
R,Up,Y,Down,Left,R,Y,Right	weapons 3 (mine, chainsaw, revolver, flamethrower, carbine, smg, dual-barrel)

Code	Effect
R,Up,X,Down,Left,R,X,Right	weapons 4 (flashbang, bat, pistol, rpg, carbine, micro smg, stubby shotgun)

GameBoy Advance

Grand Theft Auto ADVANCE

Activate Cheat Mode

Code	Effect
While playing press A + B + Start	Activates cheat mode, displays coordinates.

Cheats to use in Cheat Mode

Enter Cheat Mode (hold down A + B + Start) then do these cheats in game, without pausing.

Preferably, you should have your fists equipped, so you don't accidentally blow yourself up or anything.

Code	Effect
LEFT, RIGHT, UP, DOWN, L, L	$15,000 Cash
LEFT, RIGHT, UP, DOWN, A, A	All Weapons
LEFT, RIGHT, UP, DOWN, A, L	Armor
LEFT, RIGHT, UP, DOWN, B, B	Health
LEFT, RIGHT, UP, DOWN, A, R	Lower Wanted Level
LEFT, RIGHT, UP, DOWN, R, A	Raise Wanted Level
LEFT, RIGHT, UP, DOWN, B, R	Toggle Gang Hostility
LEFT, RIGHT, UP, DOWN, R, R	Wanted Level Max or Zero

Level select

At main menu press: Left, Right, Up, Down, L, R, Hold start and press A. This will unlock a option that displays all the levels

Mobile

Grand Theft Auto 3

You need to install the virtual keyboard or game keyboard to enter the cheats

After installing Please use the cheats of PC

Grand Theft Auto Vice City

You need to install the virtual keyboard or game keyboard to enter the cheats

After installing Please use the cheats of PC

Grand Theft Auto SanAndreas

You need to install the virtual keyboard or game keyboard to enter the cheats

After installing Please use the cheats of PC

Printed in Great Britain
by Amazon